D1622660

2 = 4/8/04

The Quality of Courage

MICKEY MANTLE

AND ROBERT W. CREAMER

UNIVERSITY OF NEBRASKA PRESS
LINCOLN AND LONDON

© 1964 by Bedford S. Wynne, Trustee of four separate trusts for the benefit of Mickey Elven Mantle, David Harold Mantle, Billy Giles Mantle, and Danny Murl Mantle
Introduction to the Bison Books Edition © 1999 by the University of Nebraska Press
All rights reserved
Manufactured in the United States of America

♾

First Bison Books printing: 1999
Most recent printing indicated by the last digit below:
10 9 8 7 6 5 4 3 2 1

Library of Congress Cataloging-in-Publication Data
Mantle, Mickey, 1931–
The quality of courage / Mickey Mantle.—Bison Books ed.
p. cm.
Originally published: Garden City, N.Y.: Doubleday, 1964. With new introd.
ISBN 0-8032-8259-1 (pbk.: alk. paper)
1. Baseball players—United States—Anecdotes. 2. Baseball players—United States—Biography. 3. Courage. 4. Role models. 5. New York Yankees (Baseball team) I. Title.
GV865.A1M317 1999
796.357′092′2—dc21
[B]
98-31558 CIP

Reprinted from the original 1964 edition by Doubleday & Company, Inc., Garden City NY. This Bison Books edition follows the original in beginning the introduction on arabic page 11; no material has been omitted.

*To the memory
of my father
Elven "Mutt" Mantle
and to my sons
Mickey, Jr.
David
Billy
Danny
I hope that each of
them will grow to be as
brave a man as he was*

Introduction to the Bison Books Edition

Robert W. Creamer

It pleases me that my byline is on this book at last. I began working with Mickey Mantle on *The Quality of Courage* early in the 1963 baseball season. The idea for it originated with Doubleday & Co., the publishing house. John F. Kennedy's *Profiles in Courage* had been a success a few years earlier, and Doubleday felt a book on the subject by Mantle would have similar appeal.

Mantle had shown notable courage a year and a half earlier in 1961, the season when he and his New York Yankee teammate Roger Maris challenged Babe Ruth's home run record. Mickey finished with 54 home runs to Roger's record-breaking 61, but before the end of the season he was sidelined with a badly infected hip that put him in the hospital for a few days. He was back in uniform for the World Series but was unable to play the first two games. Before the third game, with the Series tied at a game apiece, and despite the fact that the incision had not healed, Mickey told Ralph Houk, then manager of the Yankees, that he was ready to play.

"He had a hole in his hip this big around," Houk told me years later, amazement in his voice. "I couldn't believe it. I said, 'God damn, man, you can't play with something like that.' He said, 'I'm playing.' I asked the team doctor if he could play and the doctor said, 'I don't see how he can with the pain he'll feel when he moves.'"

Mantle insisted on being in the lineup and he got through the third game without obvious trouble as the Yankees won. In the fourth game, however, he ran so hard trying to beat out a ground ball in the second inning that the wound reopened. Two innings later, when he again ran hard to first base on a base hit that set up what turned out to be the winning run, blood began to soak through his uniform.

"I took him out," Houk said. "He went into the clubhouse and they put another dressing on it, and after a while he came back and sat on the bench and rooted the rest of the game. Mickey was something else. Damn, I couldn't believe he could play with something like that in his leg."

So the tone, the courage, was there; Mantle was a good choice. Now he needed a writer to work with, a ghostwriter. John F. Kennedy's book had been ghostwritten. Someone had sat and talked with JFK and put the book on paper anonymously—only Kennedy's byline was on the cover—and the Mantle book was to be done the same way. Ed Fitzgerald of Doubleday, who had been editor of *Sport* magazine, knew me and the baseball stories I had written for *Sports Illustrated*, and he asked if I'd like to be Mantle's ghost. I had never written a book before, and I jumped at the chance, even though I wouldn't have a byline.

As a baseball writer I had been around Mantle for several years, but I didn't really know him, and he didn't know me. He didn't much like sportswriters, especially during his first ten seasons in the majors (1951–1960). His relations with the media had become much friendlier during the 1961 season when Roger Maris began to be subjected to daily onslaughts by writers and photographers and broadcasters. That was a new experience for Roger, and he didn't like it, but Mantle evolved into something of an elder statesman, talking more freely with reporters while counseling Maris on how to handle the pressure. His popularity with both the media and the public soared that season.

Even so, in 1963 he was still distant with writers he didn't know well, and I was one of those. Doubleday had made the arrangements for the book with Mantle's lawyers in Dallas—this was before the age of omnipresent agents—and he and I had not met beforehand to discuss the project. When I went to Yankee Stadium and introduced myself to Mickey as the writer assigned to do the book with him, he was not very cooperative. He was polite enough but withdrawn and at first not very friendly. He avoided getting started. He put off meetings. He was obviously reluctant to sit down and talk.

I might have despaired, maybe even given up the assignment, if it had not been for a story I had read on Mantle that Gerald Holland had written for *Sports Illustrated* half a dozen years earlier. In 1956 Mantle won the Triple Crown and the Most Valuable Player award, and after the season Holland was to do a feature on him. Mickey was at his most difficult in his dealings with sportswriters. He'd often respond to questions with curt, monosyllabic answers, or silence, or even by turning away.

When Gerald Holland caught up with him in the off-season Mantle was traveling from town to town being honored at one sports banquet after another, yet Holland encountered the same cold attitude. "You again?" was about the friendliest thing Mantle said whenever Gerry tried to talk to him. A shrewd man and a veteran journalist, Holland sensed that for all his success Mickey was still a country boy at heart with a country boy's inbred suspicion of city slickers, strangers who pushed their way too close, who started conversations and asked questions as though they were old friends. In the pre-television, small-town world Mantle grew up in you were cautious with strangers.

Holland realized he had to wait, and he did, patiently and quietly, as he trailed after Mickey from city to city and eventually back to his home town in Oklahoma. Mantle was innately polite despite his surface brusqueness, and in Oklahoma he would gruffly invite the writer, who was far from home, to come along when he had lunch or dinner with friends. Holland went but said little and kept his part of the table talk to a minimum. Finally Mickey turned to him and said, "Well, are you ever going to ask me anything?" He had accepted Holland at last, and Gerry got a first-rate story.

I remembered that and endured the delays until Mickey felt comfortable enough to talk with me, and from then on there was no difficulty. We usually met in his suite at the Hotel St. Moritz overlooking Central Park in New York City. He was insistent that his book tell about his father, Elven (Mutt) Mantle, who died of cancer after Mickey's first season in the majors. Everyone interested in Mantle's career knows the story of what happened between father and son in the summer of 1951, Mickey's rookie year, after the Yankees sent him back down to the minor leagues for a while. In those days being sent to the minors was a blow. Young players did not shuttle back and forth from Triple A to the majors several times a season, the way they often do today. A demotion to the minor leagues was just that, a demotion, and Mantle was demoralized by it. He phoned his father to bemoan his fate. The elder Mantle immediately drove up from Oklahoma, but instead of comforting his unhappy, 19-year-old son, he chastised him for giving up on himself. It was a turning point in Mantle's life. He stopped feeling sorry for himself, began hitting well and soon was back up with the Yankees, this time for good. Mickey always remembered what his father had done for him, and that his father never told him he was suffering from the cancer that killed him several months later.

"My father was the bravest man I ever knew," Mickey said in our first long meeting, an opinion he continued to express for the rest of his life. He was impressed by courage—quiet courage like his father's as well as headline courage—and liked doing a book about it. We traded stories, and those we liked best, those that delineated the courage Mickey admired, we included in the book.

When *The Quality of Courage* was finished and in publication I took a copy to Yankee Stadium and asked Mickey to autograph it for my children. I had come to respect his intelligence and perception, qualities I had not previously realized he possessed, and his sometimes sly, subtle sense of humor. He took my copy of the book, sat down, and with almost no hesitation inscribed it. I thought he would jot down something like "Best regards, Mickey" and let it go at that. Instead he carefully included the names of all five of my children, wished them well, and above his signature wrote, "From the man who taught your father a few lessons in journalism." I thought that was pretty good. And true.

CONTENTS

Contents

Introduction

Like all ballplayers, I am asked dozens of times each year to speak at Little League banquets and Boy Scout meetings and Father and Son dinners and I don't know how many other affairs where boys are the main part of the audience. I have to turn down most of the invitations, but I wish I didn't have to, even though as a rule I hate to talk in public. But any man who is the father of four boys —I have four sons—would be happy to have the chance to talk to boys who want to listen to him and to tell them what he has learned in his life and to try to advise them on what they should do while they're growing up.

Still, I guess it's a foolish idea, trying to tell boys what they should do. I know when I was a kid I wasn't much impressed by most grown-ups when they started to tell me how I should behave. I got sort of itchy and hoped they wouldn't take too long, because all I wanted to do was go out and play. Now that I'm a man with a family and responsibility I've learned certain things about life, but when I sit around my house in Dallas with my own boys and watch them go up against some of the same problems that I faced, I wonder how I can possibly get them to listen to me when I know that I didn't do much listening myself when I was their age.

11

Except in one way. When I was a boy there was one thing I heard grown-ups talk about that I paid lots of attention to. I respected it and admired it, and I find that I still respect and admire it.

That one thing is courage. The people I have most respected in my life were people who had courage. The stories I liked best were about courage. To this day whenever I see courage around me, in a man or a boy or a woman or a girl, in anybody, in a friend or even in someone I don't particularly like, I am filled with respect and admiration.

That is why this book is about courage. It is what I want to talk about. I hope that I will be able to get across to the boys who read it some idea of what I think courage really is, and why I admire it, and why I hope they will have courage as part of their own makeup for all of their lives.

MICKEY MANTLE

Yankee Stadium, May 15, 1964.

The Quality of Courage

The Bravest Man

(*Chapter 1*)

When I was in high school we had to read a play once about a man who was sentenced to death. I don't remember too much about the play except that the man who was about to die was terribly scared and the chaplain of the prison—or somebody who had come to visit him in his cell—tried to comfort him by telling him a line of poetry from Shakespeare. I'm not much on poetry and I don't know very much about Shakespeare, but I have never forgotten the line because the prisoner on his way to his execution kept repeating it. It went, "Cowards die many times before their deaths; the valiant never taste of death but once."

The bravest man I ever knew was my father. He died the winter after my first year in the major leagues, when I was twenty and he was only forty-one. He died of Hodgkin's disease, a form of cancer like leukemia. He knew he had it. He knew it for a long time. He was a tremendously strong man but the disease weakened him so much that he was like a shell of what he used to be. He never told me he was sick, and I believe he never told anybody, until we found out about it by accident.

Here's how I learned about it. In the second game of the 1951 World Series, which was my first World Series, I fell chasing a fly ball in the outfield in Yankee Stadium, and I hurt my knee badly. I was taken home to the hotel I was living in in New York City, and then I had to go to the hospital. My father had come up from home to see the World Series and he had left the game with me and come to the hotel. Now he went with me in a taxi to the hospital. He got out of the cab first, outside the hospital, and then I got out. I was on crutches and I couldn't put any weight on the leg that was hurt, so as I got out of the cab I grabbed my father's shoulder to steady myself. He crumpled to the sidewalk. I couldn't understand it. He was a very strong man and I didn't think anything at all about putting my weight on him that way. He was always so strong. Well, the doctors took him into the hospital, too, and they examined him and then they told me how sick he was. It was incurable, they said, and he had only a few months to live.

After the Series was over and we had gone home to Commerce, Oklahoma, my wife Merlyn and I took my father up to the Mayo Clinic in Rochester, Minnesota, to see if they could do anything. They gave him treatments that eased his pain, but there was nothing anybody could do to cure him. He went home again to Commerce, but then during the winter he decided to go out to Denver. He said there was some hospital or other out there that said it could cure him and he said he thought he'd go out there and see.

He knew they couldn't cure him. But he went out to Denver so that the little kids in our family—I'm the oldest and my sister and my three brothers were all just little kids at that time—wouldn't see him wasting away, getting thinner and thinner and sicker and sicker. So he went out to Denver, and he died there. He never complained, he never acted scared, and he died like a man. That line from that play fitted him for sure: "Cowards die many times before their deaths; the valiant never taste of death but once."

My father was brave in lots of ways. I was the oldest child and I was born in October of 1931, right in the middle of the Depression, in Spavinaw, Oklahoma. Kids nowadays don't have any idea of what the Depression was like —it's just a word in the history books—and that's great. But it was a hard time to bring up a family, especially where we lived, which was one of the poorest parts of the country. Even in wealthy parts of the country, people were standing in line for food. Finding work and earning money was the hardest thing in the world to do, and keeping a family alive and fed and happy at the same time was even harder. But he did both, he and my mother (she was pretty brave, too; she had to make do without very much —she did all our cooking on a wood stove, for one thing— but we never felt we were without anything). My father never quit, never admitted defeat.

One year he traded our house in Commerce, where he was working as a miner in the lead and zinc mines we have there, for a farm out in the country. It wasn't much of a farm—we lived in Dust Bowl country and a lot of people had quit and gone to California (you've heard of the Okies, haven't you?). But he thought maybe a farm might mean a better life for us kids. The very first year he had it, there was a flood and the river came up over the farm and ruined it. My father just picked up, went back into town, and down into the mines again.

The thing is, despite all the troubles he and my mother had because of the Depression, we had a lot of fun growing up. I had a happy boyhood, and even though I probably make more money now in a year than my father made in his life, I don't know that my kids are any happier than we were. I didn't appreciate this as a boy, but as a man I am even more filled with admiration for my father—especially for his courage in the face of trouble.

He was a quiet man and even-tempered and he was well-liked, but he could get pretty mad in that quiet way of his. I remember once there was a dance that everybody went to, a country dance or whatever you want to call it, a barn dance, a square dance. All the families went to it, fathers and mothers and kids and everybody. A couple of wise guys started to make trouble for no reason at all, just to show how mean and stupid they could be, I guess. They made things real unpleasant and they were about to ruin the fine evening that everybody was having. It's funny, but I don't remember a fight or anything else, but all of a sudden there was no more trouble. My uncles told me later that my father took the two troublemakers outside and licked them both. Just like that. No fuss. No bother. He belted them, and they left, and he went back inside, and the dance went on. It got to be a story that people liked to tell when they were sitting around talking about the old days. But my father never talked about it.

He loved baseball and he always wanted me to be a ballplayer. He named me for Mickey Cochrane, the great catcher who was at his peak about the time I was born.

Actually, Cochrane had a bad World Series the month I was born, when Pepper Martin and the St. Louis Cardinals were stealing bases on him and running wild. Cochrane was criticized, but baseball men said it wasn't his fault so much as it was his pitchers', who didn't hold the runners tight to their bases. Anyway, one bad Series couldn't affect my father's admiration for Cochrane, and maybe he named me Mickey just to show people that he was still loyal to the man he admired.

When I was growing up my father used to take me with him all the way to St. Louis to see major league games. That was the nearest big league town in those days, and he and friends of his would drive six hundred miles up and back on a weekend to take in a couple of games. My father always took me with him.

I guess my making the major leagues was one of the happiest things that ever happened to my father, and I often think how glad I am that I made it before he died. Though I almost didn't.

That first year I was with the Yankees, when I was nineteen, I struck out an awful lot. Casey Stengel was the manager and he played me a good part of the time, but even though I got some hits now and then, I kept striking out. It was terrible. Finally, in July, the Yankees decided to send me down to the minors to get rid of the strikeout habit. It is a depressing thing being sent down to the minors, and I felt low. I thought I had missed my big chance. I figured they had looked at me and didn't want me.

The Yanks sent me to Kansas City, which at that time was a Yankee farm club in the American Association.

There I got even worse. I believe I got one hit in my first twenty-two at bats, and that was a bunt. My father came up from home to Kansas City to see me play. I was living in a hotel there and, boy, was I glad to see him. I wanted him to pat me on the back and cheer me up and tell me how badly the Yankees had treated me and all that sort of stuff. I guess I was like a little boy, and I wanted him to comfort me.

He said, "How are things going?"

I said, "Awful. The Yankees sent me down to learn not to strike out, but now I can't even hit."

He said, "That so?"

I said, "I'm not good enough to play in the major leagues, and I'm not good enough to play here. I'll never make it. I think I'll quit and go home with you."

I guess I wanted him to say, Oh, don't be silly, you're just in a little slump, you'll be all right, you're great. But he just looked at me for a second and then in a quiet voice that cut me in two he said, "Well, Mick, if that's all the guts you have I think you better quit. You might as well come home right now."

I never felt as ashamed as I did then, to hear my father sound disappointed in me, ashamed of me. I shut my mouth. I didn't say anything more about quitting and going home. I kept playing. Things got better and a month later the Yankees called me back up to the majors, and I've been there ever since.

I have wondered sometimes exactly what it was. I know that I wanted my father to comfort me. He didn't. He didn't give me any advice. He didn't show me how to swing the bat any different. He didn't give me any inspiring speeches. I think that what happened was that he had so much plain ordinary courage that it spilled over, and I could feel it. All he did was show me that I was acting scared, and that you can't live scared.

A year later he was dead. I realized then that he was dying when he came to see me in Kansas City, though he never gave any sign to me. He didn't die scared, and he didn't live scared.

My Friend, Mr. Ford

(*Chapter 2*)

Bravery has different forms. Sometimes it is a man facing a very difficult situation, but sometimes it is an everyday thing, a man doing his job, like a policeman or a soldier on duty along a truce line. The work is hard, but it's there every day; there is no glamor, but the problem is always there. The brave men in these cases are the ones who get the job done every day.

We have that in baseball. Some players dog it a little. There aren't too many of them, because they don't last. They don't stick in the big leagues. Their trouble is, they give in to the problems they face. Things look too big or too tough or as though they'll take too long a period of time. The trouble with some of these fellows is, they don't work hard enough. It seems funny to mention work when you're talking about a game, but I've found that it's true in every sport—the man who is good is the man who works hard at it. He sticks with the difficult thing, works at it, and beats it. The trouble with too many who don't make it is, they let themselves get beat before they start. They say to themselves, I know I can't do it, and so they quit. They beat themselves.

I like the other kind, the kind who work hard, the kind who don't quit. And my favorite is Whitey Ford.

My Friend, Mr. Ford

Whitey Ford has been a major league pitcher since 1950. He has a great deal of ability, but so do a lot of other people. I think the main reason that he has been so good for so long is simple. Whitey Ford is a brave man. Now, he'll rib me for calling him that. He'll say things like, "What are you trying to do, Slick? You trying to butter me up now that I'm a coach? You don't get any favors from me, Mantle."

He's a wise guy, all right. He's always kidding around. But it's true—he is a brave man. He gives everything he has every time he pitches, and he's at his best in the toughest games. He always has been. Even in the 1963 World Series. Remember when Sandy Koufax beat us in the fourth game to give the Dodgers their sweep of the Series? People said the Yankees had been humiliated, and there certainly was no question that we were beaten badly. But don't tell me Whitey Ford was humiliated. He pitched that last game for us. Do you know how many hits he gave up in that game? Two. He went against Koufax, the best pitcher in baseball, and he threw a two-hitter. I know pitchers who have gone out to pitch against great rivals like Koufax who were beaten before they started. You know, they feel, "What's the use?" Whitey went out that day to win. He expected to win. He pitched a game good enough to win. He lost 2–1, and the winning run scored because of an error. I felt as bad for Whitey as I did for myself and the team. He's too good a pitcher to have to lose games like that.

I have played with Whitey for more than a dozen years. He came up to the Yankees the year before I did, and then went into service for two years before he rejoined the club. Starting in 1953 we have been together on the same team ever since. I have seen him pitch a lot of ball games, a lot of clutch games, a lot of World Series games. And I have never seen him throw at a batter. It's no secret that some pitchers throw right at a batter, not to hit him (though once in a while you come up against a guy who is mean enough to try) but to make him fall down out of the way. They're trying to loosen up the batter, scare him.

I have never seen Whitey do that. He'll pitch inside tight and he'll throw hard, but he doesn't throw *at* anybody. He never tries to knock a batter down. He beats the batter with his pitches, his brains, and his control. And his guts.

Whitey always looks in charge out on the mound. They'll get the bases loaded against him, and he'll turn around and rub up the ball and look out toward center field, where I am, and he seems to be saying, "How is everything out there, Mick? Everything's under control here."

Then he turns back to work and—well, I know Whitey loses ball games sometimes. Every pitcher does. But Whitey has lost fewer games compared to his wins than any other pitcher of any importance in the history of the major leagues. He has the best won-lost percentage of all time. When he is pitching, you don't expect to lose. You expect to win. You're confident. That's the way it is playing behind Ford. He's one of those people like my father —his courage rubs off on the people around him.

I remember in one World Series we played against the old Brooklyn Dodgers, we lost the first two games in Ebbetts Field. We had lost four of the last five games to

My Friend, Mr. Ford

Brooklyn the year before, after we had won the first two games, so that meant that the Dodgers had won six of the last seven World Series games the two clubs had played. It was beginning to look as though the Yankees were washed up, and that the Dodgers were the new big team in baseball.

Whitey had been named to pitch the third game. He had started the first game and we were sort of shook when the Dodgers racked him up pretty badly. But we had to win that third game, so Casey Stengel called on Ford again. The day before, after we had lost the second game, a sportswriter asked Whitey in the clubhouse how he felt about the idea of starting again so soon after being knocked out of the box. I mean, the game coming up was a game the Yankees absolutely had to win, and the Dodgers were hitting hard and they looked red hot. The sportswriter asked Whitey whether he felt nervous and whether he thought he'd have trouble sleeping and would he lie awake wondering how to pitch to the big Dodger hitters like Snider and Robinson and Campanella and Furillo and Hodges and Reese. The writer had a point. After all, the Dodgers had scored nineteen runs off our pitching in two games. And if I know Whitey, he was thinking about that game every second, figuring what he was going to throw, wondering how he could set up this batter and how he could get that one to hit his pitch.

Well, you know how it is when somebody guesses what you're thinking when it's sort of embarrassing—like you're thinking how much you like that girl who lives down the street from you and your kid sister, or somebody, says, "I bet you're thinking about Linda," and you get sore,

25

even though they're right. Ballplayers are that way, too. They can be worrying inside about something but let a sportswriter ask about it and a ballplayer is apt to get sore. I know I do, or at least I used to. I'm not as touchy now, and maybe it's partly because of Whitey.

At any rate, instead of getting irritated at the sportswriter's questions, Whitey just grinned and began to kid the writer. He was as relaxed as a man could be. He acted as though there wasn't a thing in the world bothering him. He looked as though the game he was going to pitch the next day was about as big a problem as a fathers-and-sons game at a picnic. He seemed as sure of himself as a man could be. And I tell you, if you were on the Yankee squad that day, you would have *known* you were going to win the next day, no matter how hot the Dodgers were. That's the kind of poise and confidence, or courage, that Ford has. We felt it, too.

The next day Whitey beat the Dodgers and we were back in business. After his game we took three out of the last four and won the Series. We had a lot of heroes in that World Series. Don Larsen pitched his perfect game two days after Whitey's game, and Johnny Kucks pitched a shutout in the seventh game. Bob Turley lost a 1–0 heartbreaker in ten innings. Yogi Berra hit three home runs, two of them off Don Newcombe in the final game. I hit three homers and Billy Martin hit two, and Enos Slaughter won a game with a homer.

But there is a good argument for saying that Whitey Ford was the reason we beat the Dodgers. He had to stop them, and he did. He did it when they were hot, when it looked as though no one else on our staff could do it. After he did it, the Series swung our way.

It's an old story. When one brave man does something, others follow.

Machine Guns and Oil Lamps

(*Chapter 3*)

Bravery is a complicated thing to describe. You can't say it's three feet long and two feet wide and that it weighs four hundred pounds or that it's colored bright blue or that it sounds like a piano or that it smells like roses. It's a quality, not a thing. Lots of men have tried to describe what it is, and most of them have done pretty well, though all the definitions vary a bit.

One of the most widely quoted definitions of courage is the famous one of Ernest Hemingway's. I bet I've seen it quoted fifty different times, though at first I didn't know it was Hemingway who made it up, and I guess it's been mentioned so often that some people sort of laugh at it now because it seems so obvious. Never mind them. I think it's quoted so much because it's such a good definition of courage. Hemingway used that short common word that my father used—guts. He said, "Guts is grace under pressure."

What that means is, when you're in a tough spot you do what you have to do and you do it without getting panicky. I'll tell you a couple of stories to try to explain that.

A man I know told me about a patrol he had been on in Germany during World War II. There were about seven or eight American soldiers going in single file along the edge of a little brook that flowed down a very gradual slope out of some woods toward a group of buildings. The Americans came out of the woods and went toward the buildings. It was quiet and they didn't expect any trouble, but all of a sudden there was a burst of German machine-gun fire from one of the buildings. It was what American soldiers in World War II called a burp gun—because it fired so fast that the sound it made sounded like a belch. I mention this only to show that the American soldiers knew at once that it was enemy fire. My friend told me that as soon as he heard the burp gun he dove flat on the ground, half in and half out of the little brook, with his face down, trying to keep from being hit. He said that all he was thinking about was not being hit—except that as he went down he caught a glimpse of the sergeant who was leading the patrol. The sergeant was a quiet, red-headed man who never said much, and everybody liked him. As my friend dropped to the ground he saw the sergeant fall to his knees and he thought, Oh, gee, he's been hit in the stomach.

But as he was lying there with his face down he heard American submachine gun fire (which was slower and deeper in sound than the German gun), and when he lifted his head to look there was the sergeant, on his knees, firing his submachine gun back at the windows of the building.

What had happened was that when the sergeant heard the burp gun he half dropped to his knees for protection, which is instinct, but at the same time he reacted as the leader of the patrol and did what he had to do. He wasn't wounded, and he didn't go all the way down on his face to hide, as all the men behind him did, instinctively. He knew at once that he couldn't hide with his face on the ground because the enemy would pick off his entire patrol, one by one. So as he dropped to his knees he swung his gun up to firing position and fought back. The German fire stopped, and the American patrol scrambled for cover and were able to fight on an even basis.

What the sergeant did took guts, grace under pressure.

It doesn't have to happen only in something like war. I know some people who were skiing up in the mountains. They had a cabin and after skiing all day they would come back to the cabin in the evening and eat and sit around and talk and relax. It was a lazy, sleepy, tired time of day. This evening I want to tell you about, they had a fire going in the fireplace and food cooking on a stove in the kitchen. They had bottled gas for the stove but there was no electricity in the cabin, so they were using oil lamps.

The entrance to the cabin was through the kitchen, and there was one narrow door from the kitchen into the main room, where the fireplace was and where they were all sitting around, half dozing, half talking. Two of the men went into the kitchen to get more coffee. One of them carried an oil lamp. Now, oil lamps aren't too common now, but anybody who has ever used one knows how terribly hot the glass chimney of the lamp can get—it can burn the skin right off your hand.

The man carrying the lamp put it down on a table in the kitchen, poured coffee into the cup he was carrying and the cup the other man was carrying, and then turned to go back into the main room. He wasn't used to oil lamps.

Without thinking he reached out and picked it up by the glass chimney and turned toward the door. The other man, who knew all about oil lamps, stared at him with— I guess horror is the right word. He simply could not believe that the first man had actually picked up the lamp by the incredibly hot chimney. He told me, "It was like watching somebody walk in front of an automobile. You know there's going to be a terrible accident, but there's nothing you can do." He expected the first man to yell and drop the lamp. If he did, the lamp would fall to the floor right in the doorway to the main room. It would break and explode and catch fire in the doorway. The cabin would have gone up in flames and the people in the main room would have been trapped. Several people would have been seriously hurt, if not killed.

But the man carrying the lamp did not drop it. He had the lamp a good five feet away from the table by the time the pain from the searing hot chimney hit him. He said, "Ow!", stopped, turned, moved the lamp all the way back to the table, set it down, and took his hand away. It was covered with blisters.

"Boy, that hurts," he said, looking at it.

The other man, still stunned by the thought of the disaster that didn't happen, said, "Jim, how come you didn't drop that lamp?"

Jim looked at him. "Drop it?" he said. "It would have set the place on fire."

That is a perfect example of grace under pressure. That is doing what you have to do when every instinct says do the other thing. If Jim had picked that oil lamp off a stump outside in the snow, he would have dropped the lamp and let it break. It wouldn't have hurt anybody or anything, and the only damage would have been the cost of the oil lamp. But inside the cabin, Jim couldn't let it drop. Even though his palm was blistering from the heat, he knew instantly that he had to put the lamp back carefully on the table, no matter how much it hurt.

That man never got a medal and, in fact, the other people in the cabin never truly realized that his courage, his bravery, his valor, his guts, his grace under pressure, probably saved their lives.

I want to tell one other story to show an example of the opposite of grace under pressure, a story about a man who lost his poise in the clutch. It's a baseball story, and I think it explains a little bit of the old question: Why do the Yankees win so often?

We were in a tight pennant race and we were playing a team that was really challenging us for the league lead. I think they were actually in first place by a few percentage points when this series of games began. They had been riding a hot streak, and when a team gets that way it's important that you cool them off fast. We felt we *had* to beat them in the first game of the series. We had to show them who was boss.

Whitey Ford was pitching for us, and their best pitcher was going for them. I don't want to mention his name because he's a nice fellow and a good pitcher, and I don't want a description of one incident to sound as though I'm knocking him.

He was a pitcher who had been just so-so until he got confidence in his curve ball. Using the curve, he could keep a batter off balance. You know that some pitchers, when they fall behind a batter on the count, don't like to throw their curve because they're kind of afraid that they won't get it over the plate and they'll walk the man. Especially in a tight spot. Well, this fellow had developed into one of the best pitchers in the league because he had learned to throw the curve with a three-and-two count, or even three-and-one. He was tough to beat.

This day was no different, until the last inning. Whitey was great for us, as usual, but the other guy was just as good and we went into the ninth inning with the score tied 0–0. In the last of the ninth we got a base hit and then there was an error and a walk and all of a sudden we had the bases loaded with only one out. There we were, with the winning run on third base and a pretty good hitter coming up. (No, it wasn't me, in case you were wondering.) Our batter—I'm not going to use his name either, because he's still around—was a good fast ball hitter but he was really weak against a good curve ball. We figured the other pitcher would throw him a mess of curves, and we were worried that he would get our man to hit the curve on the ground and into a double play, which would get them out of the inning with the score still tied.

Our batter fought pretty hard at the plate and the count went this way and that, and pretty soon it was three balls and two strikes. Now there it was, a sort of classic baseball situation: score tied in the last of the ninth, bases loaded, three and two on the batter. When you're a kid you sometimes dream about dramatic situations like that. But after you've been in the majors for a while, you find out that such situations happen several times a season.

They are still tense and dramatic, but a major leaguer should not be spooked by them. He has a job to do in a situation like that, and he should do it.

We were sure that the next pitch would be that good gutty curve and that we would be lucky if our man did nothing worse than strike out or pop up. A strike out or a pop up would still leave us an out. A double play, on the other hand, would knock us out of the inning.

But you know what happened? Their pitcher got nervous. Instead of thinking of his curve and getting the batter to hit the ball on the ground into a double play, he got to thinking about what might happen if he *didn't* get his curve over the plate. If he missed it would be ball four, and the winning run would be forced in. He thought about that so much that he gave up on his curve. He was afraid to throw it. He decided that it would be safer to throw a fast ball because he knew he could get a fast ball in the strike zone. He played it safe, he thought, and threw the fast ball. And our guy, who ate fast pitches for breakfast, swung and hit a nice long fly to the outfield. The man at third tagged up and trotted home easily with the winning run.

As I said before, that pitcher was—and is—a good ballplayer and a nice guy. But that day, in a clutch spot, under pressure, he lost his nerve. He did not do what he had to do. He did the wrong thing. And it cost him. You can get away with a chicken move once in a while, but over the long run the percentages catch up with you. You have to do the right thing.

I honestly believe that that is one of the reasons why the Yankees win so much. (Now don't go bringing up the

1963 World Series, when the Dodgers beat us four straight. We didn't have a chance to lose our nerve in that series. We didn't have time to. Koufax and Drysdale and Podres and Perranoski just knocked the bats right out of our hands.) The Yankees force and pressure other clubs into clutch situations, and then the other teams, sooner or later, lose their poise. They start worrying, and then they do the wrong thing. Those wrong things are the "lucky breaks" the Yankees get so often.

In the clutch, you do the right thing without worrying about the consequences. That's courage, too.

Let the Critics Laugh

(*Chapter 4*)

I suppose just about every parent has had the experience of having a child come crying into the house complaining that somebody had called him a name. Sometimes it's a one-shot name, but other times it's a name that takes hold and becomes a nickname that sticks, a nickname that you don't like. I knew a boy once whose last name was Cotton. There was a little kids' book at that time (maybe it's still around) that was about two rabbits called Peter and Molly Cottontail. For some reason, the kids began calling this boy Molly Cottontail. Why they didn't call him Peter Cottontail, I don't know. But from Molly Cottontail they shortened it to just Molly and the nickname stuck. He hated it—I don't blame him too much—and I think he became a different guy from that time on. He thought the nickname was an insult, and he couldn't take it. He'd lose his temper and fight about it; he became a real unpleasant person. Now, you can blame that on the kids who gave him the name, of course, but I think a lot of the blame was with that boy, too. He forgot the old saying, "Sticks and stones can break my bones, but names will never hurt me."

The kid they called Molly was hurt by his name—but not really. He hurt himself by letting it bother him; the name itself didn't matter. I can hear him saying, "Oh, yeah?" And I can imagine other kids with nicknames they don't like saying the same thing. But I still say I'm right. It isn't the name. It's the person. Or didn't you ever hear of Nellie Fox?

Nellie is a girl's name, right? If names matter, shouldn't a man with a girl's nickname be upset by it? But if you ever saw Mr. J. Nelson Fox, second baseman and .300 hitter, stick a chaw of tobacco in his cheek before going up to poke a base hit or two off the best pitchers in the league, you know how much that name bothered him.

The fact is, he turned things around and made Nellie a name for a man to be proud of. When baseball fans hear the name "Nellie Fox," they don't think of it as standing for anything to be ashamed of; they think of it as representing one of the best ballplayers they've ever seen play. The man makes the name; the name doesn't make the man.

Before my time in the major leagues—in fact, way before I was even born—there were a couple of fine big league players named Bransfield and Jacobson. Bransfield's nickname was Kitty and Jacobson's was Baby Doll. On my own team right now there is Elly Howard, and while in this case Elly is just short for Elston, Elly is usually thought of as a girl's name. Except in baseball, where it stands for the Most Valuable Player in the American League for the year 1963. One of the hardest-fighting ballplayers and managers of the past thirty years has been Birdie Tebbetts. How many kids do you know who would relish a nickname like Birdie? But I'll tell you, when a baserunner trying to score on a close play at the plate banged into Tebbetts, who was one of the best catchers in the game, he didn't find himself making any jokes about the nickname. "Birdie" meant a tough ballplayer.

The greatest player who ever lived had a nickname that would have embarrassed most boys. His real name was George H. Ruth, but he was called Babe. Babe Ruth was so terrific that he changed the meaning of his nickname, so much so that big powerful hitters who came along after him were called Babe out of respect. But when Ruth broke in it was a nickname for a baby. He was just a young kid fresh out of school when he joined the minor league Baltimore Orioles in 1914, and his teammates were mostly men in their twenties and thirties. The owner of the Orioles was Jack Dunn, and when Ruth joined the team the veterans called the young player "Dunn's baby," or "Dunn's babe." The name caught on and he was called "baby" or "babe" from then on. But as I said, he turned the name into a symbol of strength and power and ability, and I guess even today a boy sort of enjoys it when he hits one over the fence and someone says, "Hey, Babe!" But remember that when Ruth broke in, it didn't mean that. He had to overcome it.

I think that kids—and a lot of adults, too, for that matter—worry too much about things like nicknames and worry too much that someone might be laughing at them or criticizing them. Boy, if you worry about everything everybody says about you, you'll never move. You'll be afraid to, because someone won't like the way you walk.

Some people are natural-born critics. They have a knack for it, like some people have for singing or drawing pictures or playing the piano. They spend most of their time finding something wrong with somebody else. They don't look at themselves, naturally; or if they do, nothing they see bothers them. But with other people, they notice right away if something is different or wrong or out of place, and they call attention to it. If you let them bother you, you can waste a lot of time and effort worrying about them. But the solution is: don't worry about them. Forget it.

I don't mean you should ignore all criticism—particularly that from parents and teachers and coaches and good friends—because some people are honestly trying to help you when they criticize something. That's called constructive criticism, and you should pay attention to it. But the other kind is just a tearing-down criticism, which has no point or reason except to satisfy the person doing the criticism. You simply can't worry about it. A motto I remember from when I was a kid, and which I don't think I really understood then, was, "Be yourself." I think what that means is—don't pretend to be what you're not in order to avoid criticism. Be yourself; improve yourself, of course, by study and practice and common sense. But don't fake it, just to keep on the good side of somebody who spends all his time picking apart other people.

Take Yogi Berra. No one has been laughed at and criticized more than he has. I don't suppose this is exactly hot news, but Yogi isn't the handsomest man in the world, and neither is he the best-educated. When he broke into baseball, a short, stocky man with a powerful build and a short neck, a fairly homely face, a deep guttural voice, and a way of speaking that didn't sound much like Harvard, the deep thinkers really got on him, the ones that couldn't carry his glove, let alone his bat. He took an awful riding, and the most difficult part was that he kept hearing the same jokes—not just for a month or so, or for one season, but for years and years and years. A guy would hang from a dugout roof by one hand and tuck up his legs and scratch himself on the side, like a monkey, and yell, "Hey, Yogi, look at me. Is this the way you do it?"

You can get pretty tired of heavy humor like that. But Yogi never let it get to him. He never got sore. He never let it interfere with his playing.

Yogi made some mistakes in things he said now and then, and they were pretty funny and people repeated them. But then they started making up Yogi stories, and after a while it got so that any story you ever heard in your whole life about someone making a mistake in manners or grammar or anything like that would become a Yogi story. He would have had to have been awake twenty-four hours a day to say and do half the things they said he did.

Despite all the bad jokes about hanging from trees, Yogi is a smart man. He's one of the shrewdest baseball men I've ever known, and he's not dumb in other ways either. He has a beautiful home in New Jersey, and he has solid business interests outside baseball. He has good business sense just the way he has good baseball sense. He's smart. When he was being ridiculed right and left, he had the sense to grin and take it and not worry about what was said. He knew that it didn't matter what they called him, or what they said. What did matter was Yogi himself, and what *he* did. Without being conceited about it, he knew that to him the most important person in the world was himself, and that's the person he worried about, not the .200 hitters who made bad jokes. I heard a man say once that an intelligent man is one who knows exactly how good he is and who knows how to use everything he has. Some men overreach themselves, and you can't blame them for at least trying. But a lot more don't try hard enough; they don't know how good they are and they're afraid to find out.

When Yogi was just a kid ballplayer in St. Louis he knew how good he was. He didn't think he was great; he didn't boast. But he knew just how good he was. He and Joe Garagiola were friends. Joe is now a baseball broadcaster, but he played several seasons in the National League with the St. Louis Cardinals and other teams. Joe likes to tell jokes about what a lousy ballplayer he was, but he was good enough to be first-string catcher on the world champion St. Louis Cardinals of 1946—and he was one of the hitting stars in the Series that year. Anyway, Joe and Yogi grew up together in St. Louis, and they both hoped to become professional ballplayers. Garagiola finally got signed to a contract by the Cardinals for a bonus of five hundred dollars (which was about as big as bonuses used to get—I know, because I signed for a hundred dollars). Yogi tried out with the Cardinals, too, but he looked awkward and clumsy, so although they offered him a contract they wouldn't give him a bonus. Well, Yogi knew that he was as good as Joe—they used to take turns pitching and catching on the same team—and he wanted the same bonus that Joe got. The Cardinals wouldn't do it, and Yogi wouldn't sign. Here he was, just a kid, turning down a professional contract with his favorite team. But he was right. He *was* as good as Joe Garagiola, and as things turned out he ended up becoming a hundred times better than Joe. It was a matter of principle. Yogi knew how good he was, and he had the courage to stick with that belief. If the Cardinals didn't recognize it, he'd play somewhere else.

Eventually, he signed with the Yankees (lucky for us) and began his great career. But when Yogi first came up to the Yanks, he was awkward for a major leaguer. He had a lot to learn, as all major leaguers do. Now, that is one thing that really gets me about kids sometimes. They will learn the first step in doing something, and then they decide that that's all there is to it, and that from now on it will be a breeze. But it isn't that way. Look. Every man who makes it to the major leagues has been outstanding in baseball all his life, from sandlots to Little League to high school to college to minor league ball. He has had to be outstanding or he would not have moved up. Anybody who makes the majors—even for one game—is an exceptionally good ballplayer. Just ask yourself how many really good players you've watched in high school or semipro ball, and then remember how many of them—the very good ones—were good enough to reach the big leagues.

The point is, anyone who gets to the majors is a terrific ballplayer but, even so, he doesn't know very much from a major league point of view. He has to start learning like a first-grader. When you reach the major leagues, it is unbelievable how much you don't know about the game you've been playing all your life. You have so much to learn, so much to find out, so much to practice. And it's the same in anything, in sport or out of it. The farther you get the *more* you have to learn, to study. But some boys get all upset and resentful because a coach or a teacher or a parent will jump on them all the time to practice, to study, to start learning the next thing you have to know. Yogi Berra was a better baseball player when he reached the majors than most boys could ever hope to be. Even so, for a major leaguer he was awkward and inexperienced. He had been playing baseball day in and day out for more than ten straight years, but he still had a lot to learn.

With the Yankees he played several games in the outfield, and he messed up a few plays. One fly ball hit him in the shoulder when he missed it. That, or something like it, has happened to plenty of outfielders the first few times they played in Yankee Stadium, but from the criticism he got you would have thought Yogi was the worst fielder in the history of the game.

The trouble was that Yogi looks sort of funny for a ballplayer; he's got short legs and long arms, and he looks like the kind of person who would be clumsy (he isn't, in case you're wondering; you ought to see him take a soccer ball and move it down a field—he's terrific, and graceful). To the crowd and to some reporters, he looked like the kind of player you would expect to drop a fly ball. Everybody hooted and laughed. Someone had the nerve to say that Yogi didn't *look* the way a Yankee is supposed to look. Listen, there is only one way a Yankee is supposed to look—good.

Plenty of players give up just a little, at least on the inside, when they start getting a good riding from the crowd or from the sportswriters. Yogi didn't. He still knew how good he was, and that meant he knew how bad he was,

43

too. That didn't upset him; he just knew what he had to learn. In spring training he began working with Bill Dickey, one of the greatest catchers of all time and a Yankee coach in those years. That's the time that Yogi said, "Bill is learning me all of his experiences," which isn't very good English but which meant what Yogi meant it to mean—that Dickey was teaching and he was learning.

He learned so well that he became the best catcher in the American League, and the only other catcher in baseball who could compare with him was Roy Campanella. Yogi was voted the Most Valuable Player in the American League three times in five years. He was great. He was quick behind the plate and smart. Once he made an unassisted double play, and if you think that's easy you ought to put on shin guards and mask and chest protector and see how fast things move around that plate.

When Yogi was named player-coach for the Yankees before the 1963 season, the same sort of people who laughed at him when he was a rookie started laughing again. They thought it was funny that Yogi—whom they still looked on as a joke, though a joke who could hit—should be a teacher and leader of players. But again, Yogi knew what he was, what he had to do, and whether or not he could handle a coaching job. He figured that he could do the job, and he was right. Then the Yankee front office told him they wanted him to become manager at the end of the year; that was a big surprise, but Yogi thought that one out, too. He'd been playing baseball, man and boy, for over twenty-five years. He'd been a topflight player on the best team in the majors for seventeen seasons. He had watched how great managers like Casey

Stengel and Ralph Houk had handled a team. Yogi reasoned that there weren't many people around who had more—or even as much—actual baseball experience as he had. He wasn't convinced that he'd be a successful manager, but he figured that he had more qualifications than most people to try. He wasn't scared of what the critics and the comedians would say. He wasn't bothered by the jokes and the hoots and the disbelief that he read in the paper. He wasn't worried about what people said; he knew that what he did would be what mattered. He wasn't afraid to try.

I hope my sons, and all boys, can understand that attitude. It is you that matters, not what people say about you. You could go back through history and find that the greatest men who ever lived were pecked at and criticized. If they believed everything the critics said about them, they would have quit before they began.

The Spark Called Courage

(*Chapter 5*)

Being brave doesn't mean being noisy. It doesn't mean acting big and brassy and knocking people down and saying, "Look how rough I am." It means doing what you have to do even when you don't want to do it. Or when it's awfully hard to do it. Or when you could let it slide and let somebody else do it. Or when it hurts to do it. Bravery covers a lot of ground.

Shakespeare said "valiant" and my father said "guts." Shakespeare was describing death and my father baseball, but they were talking about the same thing. There are a lot of words for what they were discussing: guts, valor, bravery, courage, heart, backbone, sand, spirit. If you read about a soldier climbing out of a foxhole and braving enemy fire to reach a wounded companion and carry him back to safety, it sounds right to call it "courage" or "valor." But take an ordinary situation in an ordinary life. If you're like me and you ever have to get up before the whole school at an assembly and speak, your knees are going to shake. You'll feel them shake and you're going to wonder why you can't stop them. You're going to hear your voice and wonder why it's squeaking instead of sounding normal, like it would if you were walking down the street talking to your friends.

46

In other words, you're going to be scared. If you get up anyway, shaking knees and all, squeaking voice and all, and make yourself say what you have to say, even though you'd rather be almost any other place in the world at that moment, that takes a certain amount of courage. But you probably couldn't call it "valor." That would sound sort of fake, because words like "valor" seem to belong to greater acts of bravery, like that of a soldier. But it still took courage to stand up in that assembly, didn't it? What do you call it? If valor and courage and bravery are too fancy, call it guts, even if that isn't a very polite word. But it means what you want to say.

Maybe I'm exaggerating the thing about standing up at an assembly, but kids who are scared of speaking in public will agree with me. I've known pro football players who weren't afraid of leaping high for a forward pass with a 220-pound linebacker roaring at them who were just plain petrified at the thought of getting up at a banquet and saying a few words. For that kind of person, or for the high school boy who doesn't want to get up and talk in front of a mob of students (who used to be your friends but who now look like your worst enemies), it takes courage to speak. It takes heart. It takes backbone. It takes bravery. It takes guts.

Whatever word is used to describe it, the subject of courage has interested men since the first caveman stood up to a sabertooth tiger and ended up with tiger steaks in the freezer and a tiger rug on the floor of his split-level cave. No, I'm wrong. It goes farther back, to the caveman who first stood up to the sabertooth tiger and lost. Winning isn't everything. As the man who revived the Olympics in 1896 said, fighting well is just as important. That first caveman, the one who lost, fought well, and some of his courage rubbed off on the next caveman and the next and the next, until finally the caveman won and the tiger lost.

Maybe that first spark of courage has kept burning, generation after generation, century after century, through one brave man after another, right down to today. Maybe it is courage as much as anything that moved man up the ladder above the other animals. You say that animals can be brave? Sure, they'll fight bravely, but that's an instinctive reaction common to animals, just as flinching is an instinctive reaction if the person next to you fakes a punch just for the fun of it. You react to the fake punch, and an animal reacts to danger. You flinch and an animal bites.

But courage is stronger than instinct. Suppose you and that kid you don't like on the next block have agreed to settle things with a fight after school. You don't react like an animal. You have all day to think about it. An animal doesn't think about anything but what is happening right now. You think of the trouble you are going to get into if your folks hear about the fight, or if the principal hears about it, or how you're apt to get a fat lip or a bloody nose because the other kid is bigger and anyhow his older brother has taught him how to box. You think how chicken you'll look if you don't show up for the fight.

Or maybe you know in your heart that the trouble is all your fault and the only reason you're fighting is because *you* happen to be the bigger one and you know you can beat the other kid up. Now you think about how you ought to do the right thing and apologize to the other kid, but you're afraid to because you don't want to appear yellow. You're wondering which takes more courage, fighting or not fighting.

The point is, as a human being you can anticipate trouble and be scared by it. And it takes courage to do the right thing when you're scared. But if you can recognize when you're scared—in the hundred different ways you can be scared, from having a charging rhinoceros bearing down on you to having to stand up in class and answer a question you don't think you know the answer to—and if you can figure out why you're scared and then dig up the bravery or courage or plain old guts to face up to what scares you, then you are a lot more than an animal that growls and bites out of instinct. You are a human being, and a human being that other people admire and respect.

The Man Who Wouldn't Fight Back

(*Chapter 6*)

Sometimes courage is very quiet. People who saw Jackie Robinson play baseball remember him as a hard, aggressive, noisy ballplayer who was always in the middle of every argument—when he wasn't winning a game by stealing home or driving in the go-ahead run or making a game-saving play in the field. I thought he was one of the best ballplayers I ever saw, and when he played against teams that I was on—in the World Series of 1952 and 1953 and 1955 and 1956—he always showed a lot of guts.

But he had even more courage his first year in the majors, 1947, when I was still a young high school kid in Oklahoma. That year Robinson hardly ever opened his mouth, he never argued, he didn't get into any fights, he was the quietest, politest player anyone ever saw. When you think of Jackie's natural personality—he liked action, arguments, rough games, give and take, and he liked to be in the center of the stage, talking, yelling, taking charge —you wonder how he ever was able to control himself that first year. Especially in the face of the riding he took, the things he was called.

Jackie was the first Negro player in the major leagues. When he broke in, he was all alone, the only one. Any new player takes a certain amount of kidding, and if the older

50

players don't like him for some reason the kidding can get pretty rough. When Robinson came up a lot of the older players—and some of the younger ones, as well—resented him because he was a Negro. They didn't care how well he could play ball, or what kind of a man he was. Robinson was a college man, a Pacific Coast Conference all-star in football, basketball, and track, a National Junior College record-holder in the broad jump, a well-educated man with a cultured way of speaking (when he wasn't sore!) and a fine vocabulary. He was a great athlete and a gentleman. But men who didn't have half his brains or education or ability got on his back and called him names that I cannot write down on paper, they were so bad. Terrible, insulting things. If anybody had called him one-tenth of those things five or six years later, Jackie would have gone over the stadium roof after them.

But that first year Jackie took everything. He didn't say a word, hardly, against the ones who were jockeying him. Branch Rickey, the president of the Brooklyn Dodgers, who had signed Robinson out of the Negro leagues and made him the first Negro player in organized baseball (when he sent him to Montreal in the International League in 1946) and the first Negro player in major league ball (when he brought him up to the Dodgers in 1947) warned Jackie that he could not lose his temper that first year.

Rickey told Robinson that he had to take every insult, every nasty name, every dirty play, and do it without showing anger or temper or even resentment. He had to turn the other cheek and keep it turned all season long. When Rickey told him this, Robinson didn't like it. He said, "Mr. Rickey, do you want a ballplayer who's afraid to fight back?" And Rickey shouted at Robinson, "I want a ballplayer with guts enough *not* to fight back!"

That first year was a crucial one for the Negro ballplayer. Jackie broke the color line, but if he blew his assignment—if he lost his temper, got in a fight, struck back at the men who were riding him—the barrier would have gone right back up again. Jackie not only had to prove himself as a major league player, which is a pretty tough job all by itself, as you can find out by asking any ballplayer who ever had a shot at the big leagues, but he had to prove it fast. There wasn't time for a second or third chance. If he failed the first time and had to be sent back down to the minors, Rickey's experiment would have been called a failure, and no telling how many years it would have been before another Negro got a chance. So that was a strain. But on top of that strain, if Robinson lost his temper and exploded under the daily bench-jockeying he was hit with every day, there would have been news stories and editorials saying it was too soon to break the color line in baseball, and again the experiment would have been called a bust. What a spot Robinson was in.

Jackie's natural style of play was aggressive, slam-bang, hardrock baseball, but he had to break into the majors without using that style. He could run wild on the bases if he wanted to, but he couldn't bang into people. He had to play his best game, but he had to be gentle and quiet. So the bench-jockeys called him a coward. It seems sort of funny now in light of the Robinson everybody got to know later, but that's what they called him. Yellow. Scared. Chicken. All those things. It must have galled

The Man Who Wouldn't Fight Back

Robinson, but he remembered what Rickey had told him: "I want a ballplayer with guts enough *not* to fight back!"

I've been told that all the clubs around the National League rode Robinson pretty hard, but no club was as rough as the Philadelphia Phillies. The Phils were managed at that time by Ben Chapman, who had been a hot-tempered guy when he was an active player (he was as aggressive a player as Robinson, I suppose, when you stop to think of it), and as a manager he was still quick to anger.

Chapman and the Phils were so rough in their riding of Robinson that finally Baseball Commissioner Happy Chandler stepped in, and Chapman and the Phils had to quiet down. The next time the Phillies and the Dodgers met, Branch Rickey asked Robinson to pose for a picture shaking hands with Chapman. Rickey's idea was that it would be good for baseball and might help to ease things all around.

Robinson didn't want to. The things that Chapman had called him still burned in his memory, but he finally agreed to do what Rickey asked. And then Ben Chapman refused to shake hands. He said that he was willing to pose with Robinson holding a bat, but that he wouldn't shake hands with him.

When I heard this story years later, I sort of cringed because I knew Jackie's temper and I guess I was instinctively waiting even then for something to explode. I think things like this cause as many fights as anything—where one person or side controls its feelings and agrees to be friendly only to have the other person or side aggravate

53

things all over again. It happens to kids, it happens to husbands and wives, it happens to countries.

But Branch Rickey talked to Robinson and asked him to pose anyway, and Robinson did. Jackie said he had to swallow more pride to pose for that photograph with Chapman than in any other thing he could remember. It must have taken tremendous effort to keep his mouth shut and his feelings under control, to suppress his natural personality for the future good not only of baseball but for the Negro in baseball.

But he did it. He did it all year. Ballplayers stepped on his feet at first base. They elbowed him. They said insulting things half under their breath but knowing he could hear. They came up with remarks that would have had peaceful Connie Mack red-necked and howling and ready to fight.

But old hot-tempered Jackie took it all year long. He made it. He made the big leagues and he didn't cause any trouble. He broke the ice. He broke the color line. He proved not only that a Negro could be good enough to play and star in the majors, he proved also that the presence of a Negro player on a ball field would not start fights and riots.

Other Negro players came in quickly after Robinson opened the door, and now some of the best players in the majors, some of the best players who ever appeared in the majors, are Negroes. And they got their chance because of Jackie Robinson's skill and courage. If it wasn't for Jackie Robinson you may never have heard of players like Elston Howard, Willie Mays, Henry Aaron, Tommy Davis. I think of kids like Al Downing, the fine young lefthander on the Yanks. I guess Al was only about six years old when Robinson broke into the majors, a little tiny kid. At that time, as I said before, I was in high school and dreaming of playing in the big leagues some day. But up to that time a Negro kid couldn't even dream. After Jackie Robinson made it, it was different and an Al Downing grew up knowing that the door was open for him if he could pitch well enough. And it opened the door for a great catcher like Elston Howard. In other words, Robinson's courage in 1947 made it possible for Al Downing to be a major league pitcher in 1963 and for Elston Howard to be the Most Valuable Player in the American League the same year.

There's an odd thing about Jackie Robinson. I myself was never very friendly with him, and I have found that a lot of people who knew him in and out of baseball really dislike him. He's a hard man for some people to like because he isn't soft and smooth-talking and syrupy. He's tough and independent and he says what he thinks, and he rubs people the wrong way. But I have never heard of anyone who knew Jackie Robinson, whether they liked him or disliked him, who didn't respect him and admire him. That might be more important than being liked.

Instant Courage

(*Chapter 7*)

My best pal on the Yankees during my earlier years with the club was Billy Martin, the infielder. Billy joined the Yanks in 1950, the year before I came up, and except for 1954 and most of 1955, when he was in the Army, we were very close until June of 1957, when he was traded to the Kansas City Athletics. Billy had been a very good ballplayer for the Yankees, but once he left us he never seemed the same. Maybe that was because he kept being traded. Kansas City got him from us in June. Detroit got him from K.C. in December of that year. Cleveland got him from Detroit in December of 1958. Cincinnati got him from Cleveland in November of 1959. Milwaukee got him from Cincinnati in November of 1960. Minnesota got him from Milwaukee in June of 1961. It's pretty hard to play your best when you're with seven different clubs in a four-year period.

But with us, Billy was a valuable man, a clutch player who lifted our team up in every game he was in. He was a hothead, I'll admit that. In his major league career he had a lot of fights. He had two that were beauties with Clint Courtney, the old catcher. He had arguments with managers like Casey Stengel and Charlie Dressen and Sam Mele. He had a fistfight under the stands at Boston with

Jimmy Piersall in 1952, when Jimmy was having the mental trouble that led to his nervous breakdown. When Billy learned later how sick Piersall was at the time, he felt very bad about it. "I didn't have any idea," he said. "I never would have fought with him. Maybe I did because sometimes I had a little trouble with my own nerves."

Billy was kidding a bit with that last remark, but under the kidding there was a note of seriousness. Billy was not always the relaxed, carefree guy he seemed to be. From the time he was a little boy, Billy always had to scramble and fight for everything, and sometimes it left him with a feeling of gloom and depression. He came from a poor neighborhood in Berkeley, California. His father left his mother when Bill was just a baby and the family never had much money. Billy grew up interested in baseball and not much else. He was a scrambler and a scrapper from the beginning. He got in a fight once during a high school baseball game and got thrown off the team. I saw a picture that a local photographer took of Billy in street clothes watching the team practice. It was one of the saddest pictures I ever saw.

When he broke into professional ball, he had a hard time because he was so scrawny looking. Billy is bigger than he looks—and he has real strong arms and legs—but he isn't terribly big as baseball players go. More than that, he had a very boyish looking face (he still does), a thinnish face that made baseball scouts looking for guys who could hit with power sort of ignore Bill. They never really believed in him. So he had to scramble and push and fight to convince people. He had to act twice as cocky just to get to the point where he could begin to show people how well he could play ball.

And the thing was, he didn't have a lot of natural ability. He had to use brains and hustle and sharp observation to make his skills valuable to a team. He'd argue with managers because he wanted them to pay attention to him so that he could show them what he could do. And managers like Casey Stengel and Charlie Dressen, both of whom managed him in both the minors and the majors, appreciated that attitude. He'd fight anybody who started a fight with one of his teammates, and he'd argue with an umpire who called a close play against anyone on his team, all because he wanted to win so badly, he wanted his team to win, and he wanted his teammates to win. I never knew anybody who hated to lose as badly as Billy did.

I remember after the 1955 World Series, when Johnny Podres shut out the Yankees in the final game to give the Brooklyn Dodgers their first World Series championship ever and Casey Stengel his first World Series defeat as Yankee manager. Way after the game was over, when Yankee Stadium was practically empty, Billy was still in his uniform in the clubhouse. He had tears in his eyes. He said, "We should have won. It isn't right for a man like Casey to lose. It's a shame for a man like that to lose."

This feeling of having to win used to wear Billy out. I think it's one of the things that ended his career so quickly after he left the Yankees. He needed to win, but the ball clubs he went to finished seventh and fifth and like that. I think he couldn't take the idea of losing, and that it ruined him as a player. He was only thirty-three when he was released by the Minnesota Twins.

I can remember when Billy drove himself so hard that he was playing on pure nerve. That was in 1953. He couldn't sleep, he fidgeted all the time, he couldn't eat. At one point, over a period of about four weeks, he lost almost thirty pounds—and he had weighed only about 165 or 170 to begin with. He was pretty nearly a physical wreck. Yet that year he played in 149 games of our 154-game schedule, went to bat 587 times, scored seventy-two runs and batted in seventy-five, which was pretty darned good for an infielder who was not supposed to be a big hitter. He did it all on guts, on pure hang-on courage. His batting average was only .257 that season, and when you think of his runs-batted-in total and the fact that he wasn't a power hitter, you know that just about every hit he got must have come in a clutch situation.

But "clutch" was the key to Billy. Because he was loud and cocky and aggressive, people thought he was all mouth and argument. They forgot the courage he had. The tougher things got, the better Billy played. He had the sort of spirit that reacted to a situation. Some people freeze, or feel sick, when they find themselves in a difficult spot. Not Billy. He came through. The figures proved it. I think Billy was one of the best clutch ballplayers of all time.

For instance, his lifetime batting average for regular-season play was .257, which is ordinary. In fact, it is almost exactly the average batting average for all players, from the worst-hitting pitcher to the league batting champion. In other words, Billy was just an average hitter.

But in the World Series, where you really feel the pressure, where everything is a clutch play, Billy had a lifetime average of .333, or seventy-six points higher than his regular-season average. That's for five World Series. I looked up in the record book to see how Billy's Series record compared to Babe Ruth's. The Babe was one of the greatest World Series performers ever; look it up some time and you'll be amazed at the things he did. But the Babe, in 129 Series at bats compared to Billy's ninety-nine, hit seven points less than Billy, .326 to .333.

Billy's greatest Series was in 1953, the year he almost fell apart from nervous exhaustion. We beat the Dodgers in six games that year, and that was a really good Dodger team. They couldn't stop Billy. He went three for four in the first game, including a triple, batted in three runs, and stole a base. He went two for three in the second game and hit a home run. In the third game he went one for three and scored one of our two runs. In the fourth game he went two for four, including another triple. In the fifth game he went two for five, hit his second home run of the Series, and drove in two runs. In the sixth and last game he went two for five, including a double. He didn't score in that game, the only game of the Series in which he didn't score a run, but he batted in two, one of them the winning run of the Series in the last of the ninth.

He had twelve hits in the six games, the most anyone has ever had in a six-game Series, and no one, not even in a seven-game Series, has ever had more than twelve. In five of the six games he had two or more hits. What a performance he put on! It was really fitting that Billy Martin won the Babe Ruth Memorial Trophy for being the Series' outstanding player.

But despite all that, there are two other instances that

show even better Billy's instant courage under pressure in the clutch. One came in the first game he ever played in the major leagues. It was in 1950 against the Boston Red Sox. Billy was twenty-one, a rookie. Pitching against the Yankees for the Red Sox was Mel Parnell, a really good lefthander who the year before had won twenty-five games for Boston. Billy didn't start the game but when the Yankees got a rally going against Parnell and put two men on base, Billy was sent up to pinch-hit.

Now, I don't care who he is, when a player goes into his first major league game he feels nervous. When a player pinch-hits, he feels nervous. When a player bats against a twenty-five-game winner, he feels nervous. When a player bats with two men on base, at a time when you need those runs, he feels nervous.

Here was a kid, in his first major league game, in his first major league time at bat, pinch-hitting with two men on base against a twenty-five-game winner. What did he do? He hit a double and drove in both runners. But he did something else, too. That hit of Martin's broke open the dam and the Yankees poured through. They knocked Parnell out of the box and batted around, and Billy came to bat again, in the same inning. What did he do? He singled and drove in another run. I couldn't find anything in the record books to prove this, but I believe that Billy Martin must be the only man in big league history who got two hits and drove in three runs in his first inning of major league play. It was typical.

A second and more famous example of Billy's poise and ability to rise to a challenge under pressure came in the seventh inning of the seventh game of the 1952 World

Series, a year before the Series in which Bill won the Babe Ruth Memorial Trophy. It was the Yankees against the Dodgers again (in my first six seasons I played in four Yankee-Dodger series), and I think it was probably the hardest-fought Series, game for game, that I've ever played in. Only one game, the second, was settled by more than two runs, and even that game was a 2–1 affair going into the sixth inning. Just read some of the late-inning scores in that Series: first game, 3–2 in the eighth, final score 4–2; second game, 2–1 in the sixth, final score 7–1; third game, 3–2 in the eighth, final score 5–3; fourth game, 1–0 in the eighth, final score 2–0; fifth game, 5–5 in the ninth, final score 6–5 in the eleventh; sixth game, 2–1 in the seventh, final score 3–2; seventh game, 3–2 in the sixth, final score 4–2.

There was tension in every game, and I think it got to us, finally. To everybody but Billy, that is. I know that something happened in that seventh game. We went ahead 4–2 in the top of the seventh inning; if we could hold the Dodgers in the last of the seventh, eighth, and ninth, we would win the Series.

But the Dodgers rallied in the seventh and got the bases loaded with one out and Duke Snider and Jackie Robinson coming up. The count on Snider went to three and two —and then Duke popped up for the second out. The count on Robinson went to three and two—and then, with all three Dodger base runners off with the pitch, Jackie popped up too, very, very high over the infield. What followed was one of the strangest things in World Series history. Carl Furillo, on third base, was across the plate almost as soon as Robinson swung and Billy Cox, who had been on second, was right behind him. Pee Wee Reese, who had been on first, had gotten a big jump and was rounding third and heading for the plate as the ball came down. If it dropped safely, all three runs would have been across the plate and the Dodgers would have been ahead 5–4 with just two innings left to play in the Series.

I think that when Robinson popped up for what looked like the sure third out, everybody on the Yankee team (except one) subconsciously relaxed. After all that tension, it looked as though we were home free. The ball was coming down between the mound and the first-base line. Yogi Berra, who was catching, could have caught it, but the right play on a pop like that is for an infielder to take it. But Joe Collins, our first baseman, didn't move for it. He seemed to lose sight of it. Bob Kuzava, our pitcher, could have caught it, but pitchers don't usually take pop flies and he was looking at Collins, waiting for him to take it. Suddenly, everyone realized that nobody was taking the ball and that it was going to drop safely and the Dodgers were going to score three runs—and that's exactly what would have happened if it hadn't been for Billy Martin. He realized, an instant before anyone else did, what was happening and he reacted like a cat. He sprinted forward, lost his cap as he did, lunged for the ball, stuck out his gloved hand and, running full speed, caught the ball knee-high.

It was only a simple pop fly but it was one of the great World Series catches. It was an unforgettable clutch play. And it was typical of my pal Billy Martin, who accomplished so much in baseball with his own special brand of instant courage.

The Quiet Man

(*Chapter 8*)

Many stories about courage have to do with people who have overcome physical handicaps. When you stop to think how hard it is to make good sometimes when you have everything going for you, you begin to realize how extra hard it is when things are going against you, and you gain an extra measure of admiration for the people who hang on and make it anyway.

In the 1957 World Series, when the Yankees played the Milwaukee Braves for the first time, I had a run-in at second base in the fourth game of the Series with the Milwaukee second baseman. I don't mean we had a fight, or anything. I don't think we said anything to each other, and in any case neither of us was sore. I got picked off second base, but the pitcher's throw was wild and the play ended up with the second baseman sort of hanging over my shoulder. He really shouldn't have been there but he was sort of pretending that he had leaped for the ball (which he didn't have a chance of getting). He was hoping that I wouldn't be able to make it to third base, and if accidentally falling all over me would keep me on second that was fine with him.

His name was Red Schoendienst, and in everybody's book he was one of the best second basemen ever to play the game. He had come to the Braves in June of 1957, after more than ten seasons with the St. Louis Cardinals and one year with the Giants, who were in New York then.

With the Cardinals, Red had been tremendous. He hit .342 one year, just missing the batting championship, and he seemed to be on the All-Star team every year. In 1950 he won the longest All-Star game ever played when he hit a home run in the fourteenth inning.

Red was a very quiet fellow who never said a great deal, but when Frank Lane, then the general manager of the Cardinals, traded him away in June of 1956 Red's feelings were hurt. St. Louis was his home (he grew up just across the Mississippi River in Germantown, Illinois) and he had been a Cardinal since 1945. He had been hurt and not playing his best at the time he was traded, but he was convinced he was still a big league ballplayer.

Red did a good enough job for the Giants, who were deep in the second division in 1956 when Schoendienst joined them, and who were still in the second division in 1957, when the Giants traded him to the Milwaukee Braves. But Red was the kind of ballplayer who does not show to best advantage with a second-division team. Let me explain. A slugger—a home run hitter like myself—will often look very good with a second division team. He gets a lot of good balls to hit because most of the time his team is way behind and the opposition pitchers don't worry too much about giving up an occasional home run. A slugger stands out on a weak team.

A player like Schoendienst is different. Red was a sharp hitter who could bunt, hit-and-run, move men around the bases, drive in a key run from third base. In the field, he would always make the key play, the hard out that takes a pitcher out of a rough inning, the play that often means the difference between winning and losing. On a second-division club there isn't as much chance to use Schoendienst-type skills. There isn't much point in hitting a ground ball to the right side to move a base runner to third when the score is 8–0 against you. And the great play in the field doesn't mean a thing if you're behind 13–2 in the fifth.

So a player like Red Schoendienst sort of disappears with a second-division club. I think that's what happened to Billy Martin after he left the Yankees. He was tremendous with us, and he was a Schoendienst-type player. I don't mean that Billy was as good a hitter or a fielder as Red, and I know that Red wasn't as rambunctious as Billy, but Billy's value to a team was in the many little ways he did things to help you win. He wasn't able to help a second-division team with those things. I think the same thing could happen to a player like Junior Gilliam of the Dodgers. Gilliam is one of the most valuable men the Dodgers have had over the years, and he'd be a valuable asset to any team fighting for the pennant. But put Gilliam on the Mets or the Colts, and he would have been wasted. Or, anyway, not appreciated.

When Red Schoendienst joined the Braves, he was just what they needed. The Braves had threatened for the pennant in the National League in 1953, their first year in Milwaukee. They finished second. They threatened in 1954 but finished a close third. They finished second again in 1955, and second again in 1956. They had a good team —great pitchers like Warren Spahn, Lou Burdette, and

Bob Buhl, a fine catcher in Del Crandall, terrific hitters like Henry Aaron, Ed Mathews, and Joe Adcock, a fine center fielder in Bill Bruton, and a sparkplug shortstop in Johnny Logan. But they lacked something, some little thing that kept them from winning, instead of finishing second or third.

Then Schoendienst came along. I don't know exactly what it is that Red did, but after he joined Milwaukee the Braves broke through to their first pennant, and they beat us in the World Series that year, too. Then they won a second successive pennant and almost won the Series again. They didn't have Schoendienst in 1959, for a reason you may remember but which I will tell you about anyway in a minute, and they did not win. They tied for first place but in the showdown—the playoff with the Dodgers—they lost. And while they have continued to be one of the good clubs in baseball, they never were the club they had been when Red was playing second for them.

Now, I don't necessarily think that Red was the most valuable player on the Braves in those two pennant years. After all, Warren Spahn and Henry Aaron and Ed Mathews and the rest were all pretty fair ballplayers themselves.

But Red gave them that extra pennant-winning something. He was a winning ballplayer.

When he and I banged together in that 1957 Series, I jammed my shoulder. I hurt it pretty bad and I had to sit out a couple of games. I weigh about two hundred pounds, and I'm fairly compact. Red weighed about 165 and his pounds were stretched out over a long, skinny frame. But when we jammed together, I was the one who got hurt.

I don't mean that Red was deliberately out to hurt me —please don't misunderstand me—but what I do mean is, he was tough. He never gave up. He did what he had to do, he was never afraid to do it, and he won ball games.

In 1958 Red helped the Braves win a second straight pennant, though he felt poorly through a good part of the season. He coughed a lot and had trouble breathing at times, and near the end of the season he complained of aches in his chest. He always had the habit of choking up high on his bat, so as to punch out base hits, but that year he had his hands higher than ever. Charlie Dressen said, "He's only using half a bat."

The reason was, Red simply didn't have his old strength. A week or so before the World Series he had a chest X-ray taken and it did not show anything, but it was obvious that he was not well.

In the World Series he was just great—even though the Braves lost when we came from behind to beat them four games to three. Schoendienst batted .300, hit safely in the last six games of the Series, made nine hits, three of them doubles and one a triple, and turned in some spectacular plays in the field. I remember one fielding play especially. It was on a soft line drive that Yogi Berra hit that looked as though it was going over Red's head into right field. There were two outs at the time, the score was tied 0–0, and we had a man on third.

I thought sure it was a base hit and a run for us. But Schoendienst made a great play. First, he leaped high in the air and to one side and got his glove on Yogi's liner.

He couldn't hold it, but he stopped it from going through to the outfield. The ball fell toward the ground. Red swung around as he dropped back to the ground, grabbed at the ball, and deflected it. Right then, some players would have gotten panicky, scrambled after the ball, kicked it, and let the run in. But Schoendienst simply followed the ball down to the ground, stayed with it, picked it up, and threw it to first just in time to get Yogi for the third out. That play saved a run and, as it turned out, a shutout as the Braves won, 3–0.

But the most impressive thing in that Series was Red's triple. It must have been terribly painful for him to sprint the ninety yards around the bases to third, stretching that hit. When he reached third, he was exhausted, far more than a ballplayer should be. No one paid much attention at the time, but a couple of months after the Series we learned what was wrong. Red Schoendienst had tuberculosis.

He apparently had had it all season, and it had gotten steadily worse because of all his physical activity. I have been told that the most important thing for TB is rest, but Red Schoendienst not only could not rest, he played all year long and helped his team win a pennant. Then he played seven straight World Series games and he not only played in them, he starred in them.

Red had to have an operation on his lung to correct the damaged area. He spent several months recuperating and eventually he rejoined the Braves. He played quite a few games for Milwaukee and later for the Cardinals, whom he rejoined in 1961, but he had played big league ball for fourteen seasons before he got sick, and his best playing days were over.

His career really ended in that 1958 World Series. But what an ending. He showed once and for all what kind of a man he was and what kind of a ballplayer. Seriously ill with a terrible disease, he played up to the hilt for seven games. He never quit. More than that, he never stopped producing. Think of it. Even with tuberculosis sapping his energy and his strength, he batted .300, fielded beautifully, and in that one game literally ran his lungs out to stretch a hit into a triple.

Red Schoendienst never said much. But his courage spoke for him.

Three-Foot Package of Bravery
(*Chapter 9*)

Another example of quiet courage that I like shows that you don't need size to be brave. This fellow was the son of a friend of mine, and at the time he was three years old. He hated to get his hair cut. Lots of boys don't like the barber shop when they are real small, and they'll cry and maybe kick a little, but they get over it fairly early in life. This little guy didn't. He was about a year old when he had his hair cut the first time and he didn't behave too badly, but something somehow must have happened to frighten him because the next time he was taken to the barber's he raised bloody murder. He was scared to death. He screamed. He sobbed. He hated the barber shop with every ounce of energy he had.

Now, he was not a spoiled little brat who was used to getting his own way in everything. Outside the barber shop he was cheerful and friendly and cooperative, as nice a little boy as you would ever meet.

But he was terrified of the barber's. His father told me that taking the boy to get his hair cut was such a chore that he and his wife used to try to palm it off on each other. And they always ended up delaying the visit for so long a time that the youngster's hair started to look like a girl's. They tried cutting it at home, but that never

71

worked out right. Even if the boy held still, which he seldom did, the haircut was so bad that it looked worse than it did when it was long.

When they did go to the shop, the barbers would turn pale and try to hide when this little fellow came sobbing and crying into the shop, with his embarrassed father trying to calm him down. He was four years old by this time, or close to it, but the father used to have to sit in the barber chair and hold the boy on his lap while the barber cut his hair. Still the boy would cry and sob through the whole thing.

Until one great day. In the morning the father told the boy calmly that he was going to have his hair cut that day. He figured there was not much point in waiting and then springing it as a surprise. The boy said, just as calmly, "No, I'm not." He didn't say it in a fresh tone of voice. He was matter of fact, and he said it the way you might if someone asked you if you were going swimming tomorrow. "No, I'm not," he said.

"Well," his father said. "You are, but don't worry about it now."

Later in the day the father and the son went down to the shopping center and parked, and then walked along past the stores, stopping in at one or two for a few things they had to get. The father mentioned a couple of times that they were going to stop for a haircut, too, and each time the boy answered, "No." But still no fuss.

Then they were in front of the barber shop door, and the boy froze in his tracks. He was holding onto his father's hand, and he stopped dead. The father looked down at him, but he didn't say anything. He waited. The boy's face was solemn and serious and he stared through the glass door of the shop as though he were seeing a ghost. Inside, the barbers began to mutter to themselves, each hoping he would not be the one who would get stuck with cutting the holy terror's hair.

After about ten seconds the boy said aloud, but as though he were talking to himself, "I'm going to get my hair cut." The father opened the door and they walked in. The boy's face was still as solemn as an owl's. They had to wait a few minutes and so they sat down on the chairs along the wall. The barbers peeked looks at the boy, waiting for him to start crying, and the father pretended to read a newspaper. The boy sat on the edge of his chair, staring straight ahead, not saying a word.

Finally one of the barbers, with an unhappy shrug, said, "Next." The boy turned and looked at his father, and his father nodded. The boy got off his chair and went by himself to the barber's chair, all alone, looking like a man on his way to the electric chair. But he didn't make a sound.

The barbers glanced at each other. They couldn't believe it. Nobody said anything. They were afraid of breaking the spell.

The boy climbed up and sat on the little extra seat that barbers put across the arms of the barber chair for small children. He let the barber put the sheet around him and he sat as still as a statue, his face solemn and his eyes big and round and scared, while the barber cut his hair. He didn't make a sound, not a peep, not a whimper. Once his father looked up from the newspaper and caught the boy's eye in the mirror. The father smiled and nodded, and the boy smiled weakly, just for an instant. Then his face grew serious again.

No one said a word until the haircut was finished. Then the barber said, "Atta boy! Now you can get down." The little boy took a deep breath and climbed down from the chair. His father paid for the haircut and tipped the barber and the two of them left, with the barbers all nodding and smiling and shaking their heads in wonder.

Outside the shop the boy stopped and looked up at his father.

"I got my hair cut," he said.

"You sure did," the father said proudly. "You sure did."

The father told me later that he thought it was the bravest thing he ever saw in his life, the way the boy stood up to something that had terrified him all his life. Of course, a father is prejudiced and it would be very difficult to find somebody who would want to give a boy a medal for getting his hair cut.

But stop and figure what that three-year-old kid did. He did something he did not want to do. He made himself do it. He did it all by himself.

I kind of agree with his father.

Pressure All the Way

(*Chapter 10*)

One of the seasons that I will always remember best in baseball was 1961, the year that Roger Maris broke Babe Ruth's famous record of sixty home runs in one season. That was the year the American League expanded from eight teams to ten and increased the number of games played in a season from 154 to 162. All year long there were arguments over whether or not Ruth's record could be considered broken if it took more than 154 games to do it.

Some said that a record was a record and never mind the details. When they developed the fiber glass pole, every pole vault record in the books was broken a dozen times. The vaulters in the past were just as good as the present-day ones, but that did not change the fact that the seventeen-foot pole vault is accepted as the new record.

Others argued that some baseball records were practically sacred, and that Ruth's sixty homers in 1927 was one of them. They said it would be terrible to have that record broken by a combination of the modern-day lively ball and an extended season. Finally, Baseball Commissioner Ford C. Frick said that Ruth's record would have to be broken in 154 games. If it took more than that, an asterisk

75

would be put next to the record in the record books to show that it had been made in a 162-game season.

Well, Maris hit his fifty-ninth in game number 154 and he didn't hit sixty and sixty-one until we were into those extra eight games, but don't let that bother you. He hit sixty-one homers in one season and—asterisk or no asterisk—that broke the Babe's record, once and for all. Roger won't go down in the books as a greater hitter than Ruth. He'll never take Babe's place in baseball history, because no one could. Technically, the Babe still holds the mark for most home runs in a 154-game season and supposedly Roger has that asterisk next to his sixty-one. But none of that changes the fact that Roger broke the most famous record in baseball and that in 1961 he hit more home runs than any other major leaguer ever hit in one season.

It takes a lot of skill to hit sixty-one homers, a lot of strength and, as Roger Maris would tell you, a lot of luck. It also takes a lot of courage, though Roger most likely wouldn't say anything about that. I'll explain what I mean. You know how you can do some things when you're alone by yourself—like fooling around on an empty basketball court and shooting one foul shot after another and never missing—but when people are around and everyone is watching it gets harder. Right? Remember the last time you missed a foul shot in a real game?

Roger Maris was watched by everyone all season long. Toward the end of the season everything he did or said was printed in the papers. Roger is a blunt, outspoken kind of guy. He doesn't believe in white lies, I guess. I think you know what I mean. Suppose there is someone you don't want to see for some reason. And he calls you on the phone and asks you to come on over to his house. And you say, "Gee, I can't. I have to study this afternoon." It isn't really a lie, because maybe you should study, but it isn't really the truth, because you really don't have to study. It's a white lie, so that you don't have to say something rude.

If a reporter asks a question of an athlete or a politician or an actor or anybody who is in the papers a lot, the answer is usually a little careful because it's going to appear in the paper. Suppose a reporter asks Governor Jones what he thinks about Senator Smith, right after Senator Smith has just ripped Governor Jones in a speech and you know that the Governor would like to send the Senator to the moon in a one-way rocket. The answer is usually something like, "I do not agree with the Senator, but I have the highest respect for his opinion." Or maybe, "I would rather not discuss that at this time." Or even, "No comment."

Not Roger Maris. Roger is honest and blunt and he says what he thinks. If a reporter asks him what he thinks of a man the reporter knows Maris doesn't like, Roger will say, "I don't like him," and think nothing more about it. But when outspoken comments like that got printed in 1961—when everything Maris did made news—it made Roger sound like a loudmouth and a popoff, which he isn't. All those news stories made the fans react against Roger, and since a lot of them remembered Babe Ruth and were rooting for his record to stand, it turned a lot of fans against Rog. Fans can get pretty rough—I know, I've had them on me a lot—but some of the things they yelled at Maris

77

were the roughest I ever heard. A lot of ballplayers develop a sort of callus over their ears and pay no attention to what's yelled at them. But Roger is thin-skinned. He took what fans yelled at him as personal insults, and he snapped back at them. It got to be a sort of vicious circle.

Sometimes, too, a reporter would accidentally twist a comment of Maris's and make it sound like more than Roger intended. Ballplayers are always griping about umpires in the clubhouse, just to blow off steam. No one thinks anything about it, and even if a reporter prints what is said, no one pays too much attention to it when it's in the paper. But when Roger Maris griped about an umpire in 1961 and reporters printed what he said, it made big headlines: MARIS BLASTS UMPIRES. And then the fans would get on Roger harder than ever.

Every day, reporters and photographers crowded around Maris, both before and after the game, asking dozens of questions and taking dozens of pictures. Now, a ballplayer expects that some of the time and he kind of likes it, too, especially when he's had a good day and is feeling really happy. But it doesn't happen to the same player every day. Usually it's a different one—somebody's pitched a shutout or even a no-hitter, or someone else drove in the winning run, or someone else made a game-winning catch. The attention is spread around. Also, the reporters are usually fellows who travel with the club, fellows you know and who have been with the team all season long. Maybe in a World Series, or in a really crucial regular-season series, you'll get a lot of out-of-town reporters asking questions. But, again, that only happens once in a while to any one player.

But in 1961 Roger Maris got that World Series treatment every day. Every day before the game and every day after it, reporters and photographers jammed around him, taking the same pictures and asking the same questions he had been asked a dozen times before. Practically everything he said was printed somewhere, every comment, every casual remark.

You don't think that's so tough? Try to understand what he went through, what it was like. Imagine that every day before you go into school, after you have finished signing your name thirty or forty times for all the kids who surround you as you get off the school bus, you are pinned to a wall by fifteen or twenty reporters from big-city newspapers asking you how you expect to do in your English class that day. Imagine them sitting there watching you in class, watching every word you write to every question in an exam—and imagine thousands of other people cheering you or booing you each time you write something down. Imagine the reporters surrounding you again as soon as you came out of the school and asking you why you gave certain answers to the questions you were asked. "How come you wrote 'He ain't' instead of 'He isn't' in that English quiz?" one reporter asks. How do you answer him? Do you say, "I guess I'm stupid"? Then imagine a fresh batch of reporters coming up fifteen minutes later and asking the same questions all over again. Imagine a radio man and a television man interviewing you on the air about the school and the teachers and the exams. Imagine doing this every day, day in and day out, for weeks on end, and imagine not only getting passing grades but straight A's. If you happen to say one day,

"Boy, that Miss Evans sure gives rough exams," a reporter will ask, "Do you think she's unfair?" If you say, "Well, some of the questions could have been a little easier, I think," imagine how you would feel the next day to see headlines in the big-city papers saying: BUD BROWN CHARGES UNFAIR TREATMENT and BROWN BLASTS MISS EVANS.

You think I'm exaggerating? I'm not. That is the way it was for Roger Maris through the whole last half of the 1961 season. And he wasn't an actor or a politician who is used to being on stage, so to speak. He's a small-town boy, like me, and he doesn't do an awful lot of talking. Yet he had to handle a press conference every day, along with trying to break Ruth's record. If he didn't hit a home run, someone would be sure to ask, "How come you didn't hit any homers today?" Now, how do you answer a question like that?

Roger was under so much pressure and it was so much of a mental strain that his hair started to fall out. Honest. One spot on his head started to lose its hair, and Rog finally went to a doctor. The doctor said it was nerves, and that the hair would grow back when the pressure stopped. (It did, too, after the season was over.)

But through all this, Roger kept on hitting home runs. If you check the records, you'll find that several hitters made a good run at Babe Ruth's record in the past but that they fell short in September. One reason was that September was Ruth's best month—he was really hot toward the end—and a man challenging him has to pick up his own pace those last few weeks of the season. You can't coast. You have to get better. A second reason is the pressure. Every time you come to bat that last month everyone is anticipating a home run. And you know it. You start to tighten up. You start trying too hard. And you lose your rhythm and timing.

Maris was under more pressure than anybody, but he never tightened up, at least not on the ball field. He wanted to break Babe Ruth's record—any athlete would have wanted to—and after all the argument about 154 versus 162 games he particularly wanted to hit sixty home runs in 154 games.

After 153 games Roger had fifty-eight home runs. He really had hit fifty-nine but he lost one homer when a game we had played in Baltimore in July was rained out before it became official; the home run he hit in that game didn't count. We played our 154th game in Baltimore. I don't know whether you have ever been to a ball game in Memorial Stadium in Baltimore, but it is a big park, a tough one to hit homers in. Roger had hit only one there all year, the one that was washed out by the rain, and he needed two this night to reach sixty. Baltimore was Babe Ruth's home town, and the fans there were rooting for the Babe's record to stand alone. The Orioles had one of the best pitching staffs in the league that year. And it was a night game, which favors pitchers over hitters. The odds were all against Maris.

He didn't make sixty. He only hit one homer to bring his 154-game total to fifty-nine. But that night he showed courage and determination that I'll never forget, an ability to do his absolute best under great pressure.

The first time up he hit a line drive hard to right field. It was caught for an out, but just a couple of feet higher and it would have been a home run. In the third inning he did hit a home run, a four hundred-foot drive to deep right field. That was no. 59, and now he needed one more to tie Ruth's record. In the fifth inning, with two strikes on him, he hit another line drive deep to right field, but it curved foul, and then he struck out. In the seventh inning, with one strike on him, he hit a long, long fly down the right field line, but again it went foul. With two strikes on him now, he swung again and hit a high fly deep to right center. It, too, was caught. If he had pulled it more to the right it would have been a home run. If it had been hit a little lower, a little more on a line, it would have carried over the fence for a home run. In the ninth inning, against Hoyt Wilhelm, the knuckle-ball pitcher, Maris pulled away from a pitch but the knuckle ball bobbed and weaved and hit Roger's bat and rolled back to Wilhelm, and Roger was out.

He didn't hit his sixtieth that night. But what a try he gave it. Even the best home-run hitters average about ten at bats for every homer they hit. That night, in five at bats, Roger hit five long drives that could have been homers (one, of course, was a homer). It was one of the greatest displays of power hitting that I ever saw, and it came at the absolute clutch moment. He didn't have much luck that night, but he had all the rest—skill and power and all the courage a man could want.

He hit his sixtieth and sixty-first when we were playing those extra eight games, and passed Ruth's record. We were all very happy about that, but I think the Yankees were even prouder of Roger that night in Baltimore than when he finally did go ahead of the Babe. We knew what he had been through all season, and we knew the pressure that was on him that night. We knew how much he wanted no. 60 in that game, game no. 154. I think the try he made, the courage he showed that night, meant more to us than all the home runs he hit.

Babe Ruth was a better home run hitter than Roger, I guess. But he couldn't have had more guts.

Nothing But Guts

(*Chapter 11*)

Don Zimmer is a stocky little guy who never made it real big in the major leagues, but he has hung around for a long time—and he has been a good, useful ballplayer. He was with three pennant-winning teams, and twice he was on the winning side in the World Series. He made it as a ballplayer because he had ability, of course—he was a terrific shortstop prospect when he was a minor leaguer, and he could always hit a ball a long way—but he did it even more on sheer guts. Few people anyplace have had more bad breaks, really bad breaks, than Zimmer has had, and fewer still have come back the way Don has.

He worked his way up through the Dodger minor league chain and went to spring training with the Dodgers in 1953. He was sensational that spring in Florida. He hit .365 and I think that was the best spring average on the club that year. But Pee Wee Reese was the Dodger short-stop at the time, and he was still at the top of his form. No rookie was going to bump Pee Wee out of the starting lineup. Billy Cox was playing third that spring, and until Cletis Boyer came along Cox was about the best-fielding third baseman I ever saw. Junior Gilliam was in his first year as the Dodger second baseman, and went on to win the Rookie of the Year award that season. Jackie Robinson

84

had moved to the outfield, but he was ready to move back to the infield any time he was needed. The only place for Zimmer was on the bench, but the Dodgers thought too much of his ability to waste him there. So they sent him to St. Paul in the American Association, where he could play every day and be available if the Dodgers needed him.

Zimmer was great at St. Paul. In early July, after he had played eighty games, he was hitting an even .300 and was leading the league with twenty-three home runs. Then, in the first inning of a night game against Columbus, when it was still twilight and hard to follow the ball, Zimmer lost sight of a curve ball. He ducked but the ball hit him on the side of the head.

He was unconscious for eleven days. The doctors had to drill two holes in his skull to relieve the pressure caused by the terrible concussion. When he came out of it finally, he couldn't even recognize his wife. He couldn't talk. He came out of it slowly, but he was in the hospital thirty-one days and spent the rest of that season recovering.

Everyone wondered if he could come back from it, and what a shame it would be if such a brilliant young player should have his career end so abruptly. No one really believed that he would come back, though, at least not far enough to make it to the majors. They thought he might try, but that he would get discouraged and give up. They didn't know Zimmer. Billy Herman, who was a Dodger coach in those days, said, "If anybody can do it, Zimmer can."

The following spring he was in training with the Dodgers again. He had a hard time. He fielded well enough, but batted poorly, under .200. He had bad head-aches, too, and though the doctors said that the headaches were not the result of the injury, the worry was there. But Zimmer hung on.

That season he got into only twenty-four games with the Dodgers and hit only .182. He went to spring training again the next year, looked and felt better, and got into eighty-eight games during the regular season, lifting his batting average to .239. Reese was getting older, and Billy Cox was about through, and it looked as though Zimmer was ready for his big chance. He went to Puerto Rico in the off-season to play winter ball and really work himself into top shape. But one day a fast ball came at his head, Zimmer threw up his arm for protection, the ball hit it, and his wrist was fractured in two places.

Eventually the wrist healed, and Zimmer was back with the Dodgers, trying again. He worked himself back into top condition and one day, finally, he made the starting lineup. After all those years, he was a Dodger regular. Then, incredibly, it happened again. He was hit with a pitched ball flush in the face. His cheekbone was frac-tured and, even worse, the doctors were afraid that the retina of his eye had become detached. Zimmer had to lie flat on his back, not moving. He had to wear dark glasses that covered both eyes completely so that he could not see, except through pinhole openings directly in front of each eye. This was to keep him from moving his eyeballs.

This would have frustrated anyone, and you would think that Zimmer, who has a flaming temper when he gets aroused, would have blown his stack right through the hospital roof. But he just asked his doctors what his chances were of playing ball again. The doctors said that if he obeyed their orders and kept as still and quiet as he could, the eye would be perfectly okay, certainly good enough to play baseball again.

So Don held still. He made himself. When he finally was allowed to get up and move about he still had to wear his pinhole glasses for a while. Later on, when he was allowed to abandon the glasses, he still was not supposed to bend over, or go for a ride in a car, or even pick up one of his little children for a hug.

He followed the doctors' orders faithfully all through that summer and the off-season, and in the spring of 1957, when he reported for training, he was fine again. He looked good and he said he felt perfect, but people worried. He'd been hit so often. Everyone sort of thought that he'd have to be a little gun-shy up at the plate.

Early in March the Dodgers played an exhibition game against the Detroit Tigers in Miami. Jim Bunning was pitching for the Tigers. A couple of fellows on the Detroit club told me what happened.

"Bunning was wild," one Tiger said. "It was his rookie year and he was really throwing hard, trying to impress the manager, and now and then a pitch would get away. Early in the game a fast ball took off and went right for Pee Wee Reese's head. Reese threw his arm up and the ball hit, and Pee Wee dropped like a rock. We all thought he'd been hit in the head. I mean, that ball was thrown *fast*. But Pee Wee rolled over and came up holding his arm. It wasn't busted, but his arm was a mess, one big bruise. He didn't play again for two or three weeks."

"So the Dodgers put Zimmer in at shortstop in Pee Wee's

place," the second Tiger said. "Zip ran for him—when Pee Wee was hit by the pitch—and then went into the field. A couple of innings later he came to bat himself. Bunning was still pitching and still throwing hard. What the heck, he was a rookie trying to win a job. I believe his control got a little better after he hit Reese."

"Not too much, though," the first Tiger said.

"Well, no. Not too much, I guess. I know that when Zimmer came up to bat against Bunning I couldn't help thinking about the beanings he had had, the holes they had to drill in his head, the cheekbone, his eye. You think about things like that. And then—I forget what the count was—*zoom!* There goes a fast ball, taking off for the moon. It just sailed, right at Zimmer's head. He ducked and went down in the dirt. I think everybody there, everybody in the stands and every player on both teams, thought he'd been hit in the head. I thought he was dead. I know I got scared."

The first Tiger said, "But old Zimmer, he hopped right up on his feet and jumped back into the batter's box, waving his bat, waiting to hit. I tell you, if I was Zimmer, I would have been about ten feet away from the plate, ready to duck again."

"But you know what happened?" said the second Tiger. "Zimmer swung at the next pitch—the very next pitch, a curve in tight—and he hit it over the left field fence for a three-run home run."

"I never saw anything like it," the first Tiger said. "I tell you, it was the only time in all the years I've played ball that I felt like cheering when a man on the other team hit a homer."

"I felt the same way," said the other Tiger. "You just have to admire a man with guts like that."

And Don Zimmer stuck in the majors, put in more than ten seasons with the Dodgers, the Cubs, the Mets, the Reds, and the Senators. He has never been a great star, but don't let anybody ever tell you that he wasn't big league all the way.

The G.I. Mustache

(*Chapter 12*)

As the Detroit players pointed out, you have to admire courage like Don Zimmer's. But sometimes kids admire toughness that isn't anything at all like the way Don Zimmer is. They admire phony courage. Because another kid acts tough, he is looked upon as something special. Even the word "tough" has come to mean something good, something to be admired. But it doesn't take courage or even toughness for a gang of kids to jump on one or two kids, or a grownup, and beat them up.

Because that's not bravery. And it's not toughness. It's mass cowardice. Every member of the gang is scared, scared that other people don't think he's much good. He thinks he's proving he isn't scared by doing something ugly to someone else. What he wants is everybody to approve of him. He's scared of how he'd feel if he thought the other kids didn't approve of him. Scared kids gather together in gangs; not teams—gangs. A team is where a boy can prove his courage on his own, on what he can do himself, or on what he can contribute to the team's good. A gang is where a coward goes to hide.

Boys sometimes get the wrong idea of what bravery is. They see people in the movies or on television doing something daring and exciting, and they think that's the only way to show real manhood. But real courage, bigger than anything you could ever see in a movie, can be found right in your own neighborhood. If a gang of kids is picking on one boy, and the boy fights back, who is braver? The gang? Or the one boy? If one member of the gang sees that it's not fair and decides to help the boy instead of beating him up, who is braver then? The rest of the gang? Or the one member who takes the risk of getting himself beat up to help somebody who needs help? That is real courage, as real as it ever can be, anywhere, anytime.

You do what *you* think is right, what you *know* is right, without even thinking twice about it. That's courage. And it's not hard to do.

You don't need a cowboy hat and a horse and a six-gun. You don't need to be a handsome private eye in a cool sports car. You don't even have to be a combat soldier.

A friend of mine who was in World War II told me this story. He said, "I was in combat when I was in the war, but I wasn't any hero. I was shot at and I shot back. I did a couple of things that sound courageous now, looking back at it. I went out and rescued a wounded man once, and another time I went out under fire to a knocked-out tank to get a machine gun we needed. But, honest, those are things you do, like catching a fly ball against the wall in baseball. You don't think about it. You just do it. There's nothing heroic about things like that. The heroes in the war did real things.

"But there was one time during the war when I did something that I think was brave, and I was proud of myself for doing it. We weren't even overseas yet. We were in a nice safe camp right in the middle of the U.S.A. We were mostly pretty young guys in my outfit, and we were sort of rambunctious. A couple of the fellows who had heavy beards, guys who had to shave twice a day if they had a date at night, grew big thick mustaches. There was no rule against mustaches in that camp at that time.

"Now, there was a guy in our barracks, a thin, sort of mean-looking fellow, who nobody liked very much. I don't know why. He just rubbed people the wrong way. Well, he came back from a ten-day furlough this one day and he was sporting a mustache he had grown when he was home. It was a scraggly little thing, sort of simpering across his upper lip. It was about the puniest excuse for a mustache I ever saw. When he came in the barracks everybody hooted and hollered and laughed, but he kept it. After a couple of days, several of the jokers in the barracks got together and decided that they would shave off Jonesy's mustache. Things like that happened all the time. One time they shaved off one of those great big thick mustaches. But the guys who were getting shaved, or got their hair cut, were usually friends of the fellows doing the shaving or the cutting, and everything was taken in good spirits. Even though the fellow who lost his mustache or got his hair cut swore he'd get even. But it was like a big joke.

"With Jonesy it was no joke. He was in no mood to cooperate. He told them to stay away from him. They said, okay, but that he'd have to shave it off himself then. Jonesy was scared. He was really scared. But he shook his head. He said he wasn't going to shave it off. The guys said, 'Well, Jonesy, we'll have to do the shaving for you then.'

"I was watching all this, laughing, I guess, when all of a sudden I realized that things were getting sort of mean. It wasn't a joke any more. Here was a whole barracksful of men picking on one poor, skinny, little guy. I wasn't built too big myself then, but before I knew what I was doing I walked up to where they were closing in on Jonesy and I told them to leave him alone. It was a funny feeling, because all of a sudden these guys didn't seem like my friends any more. Neither was Jonesy; I still didn't like him.

"One of the guys said, 'What's it to you?' I said, 'Just leave him alone. He's not hurting anybody.' Another guy said, 'You're going to stop us from shaving it off?' I said, 'I'm going to try.' The first guy said, 'You want to fight to keep us from shaving it off?' I said, 'No, I sure don't.' Another said, 'Come on, Bill. You think that mustache looks good on him?' I said, 'No, I think it looks silly as the devil.' The first guy said, 'Well, what are you doing? Is Jonesy some special friend of yours?' I said, 'No. But it's his face, and if he wants to grow a stupid-looking mustache on it, that's his business. You have no right to shave it off or to make him shave it off.'

"I guess I was pretty scared, because I remember how my voice shook, and I swear I almost felt like crying. But, you know, they backed off and let Jonesy alone. I didn't say anything to him, and he didn't say anything to me. For a couple of days I got a lot of wise remarks, but they petered out after a while. Jonesy wore that foolish mustache for a week before he couldn't stand it himself any more and shaved it off on his own.

"Maybe I was wrong. Maybe I poked my nose into something that wasn't any of my business. But I don't think so. I had just as many friends after a while as I always did. And I felt a lot better."

They Shot His Leg to Bits

(*Chapter 13*)

In the spring of 1941 a seventeen-year-old pitcher began to attract the attention of baseball scouts in the South Carolina area. He was a lefthander, big and tall and powerful, and he had a great fast ball. The Yankees tried to sign him up and so did the Dodgers and several other teams. His name was Leland Brissie, though most people called him Lou, and he turned out to be just about the bravest man ever to play major league baseball.

He didn't sign a contract with anyone in 1941 because of three men. One was his father. The second was the baseball coach at Presbyterian College in Clinton, South Carolina, a man named Chick Galloway. The third was the manager and owner of the Philadelphia Athletics, a man named Connie Mack. Mr. Brissie wanted Lou to go to college. So did Chick Galloway, and he wanted Lou to go to Presbyterian College. Both Mr. Brissie and Chick Galloway wanted Lou to play professional ball later on, after he finished college, and they both wanted him to play for Connie Mack and the Athletics.

Galloway had been a major league shortstop for the Athletics years before, and he had a deep admiration for old Mr. Mack. Mr. Brissie also admired Mack. One day Galloway took Lou up to Philadelphia and got him a try-

95

out with the Athletics. Mack was impressed and when he heard the background of the trip he arranged things so that Brissie could go to college and play ball for Galloway, with the understanding that Lou would join the Athletics when his college days were over.

So Lou Brissie went to Presbyterian College. That year, on December 7, 1941, the Japanese bombed Pearl Harbor and the United States entered World War II. Brissie finished out his freshman year, played some ball the following summer, and went back to college in the fall. But halfway through his sophomore year he enlisted in the paratroops. A year later he was in Europe, and he parachuted into southern France in the summer of 1944. He injured his back doing it, not badly, but enough so that he was not permitted to jump again. He was transferred into the 88th Infantry Division. That winter, on December 7, the third anniversary of Pearl Harbor, he was leading a squad of a dozen men (Lou was a corporal) in the mountains of Italy when a German shell exploded right at his feet. Every man in the squad was killed except Brissie. He was closest to the shell, but by an odd trick of fate he was saved because he was so close. He caught the burst in both legs but the others were hit higher up, in the chest and head, and were killed instantly.

Brissie tried to get to his feet but couldn't. He crawled about fifty feet to a small creek, and that was as far as he could go. He lay there for six hours, half in the water and half out. Years later, talking to a newspaperman, Brissie said, "I was conscious most of the time. All I can remember thinking was, I don't care how hard I've been hit; just don't let them hit me again. Only I said it in the form of a prayer. Some of them may tell you different, but when the shells were flying you said everything in the form of a prayer."

The medics finally found him and Brissie was carried back to the battalion aid station and then to an evacuation hospital. His right foot had been broken. His left foot was broken. His left ankle was broken. His left leg below the knee was shattered—he had a compound fracture (where the broken bone tears through the skin) and arteries, nerves, and muscles were badly torn. In the evacuation hospital the doctors examined Brissie's leg and discussed whether or not it should be amputated at once. A doctor explained to Lou that amputating it below the knee might save the entire leg from being amputated later.

Brissie was in extreme pain but told the doctor that he was a ballplayer and that he hoped to play professionally and that he had a chance for the big leagues. He told the doctor that if his leg was amputated he would never be able to make it. He begged them not to amputate. He asked them to try to save it if they possibly could.

The doctors tried. They did what emergency work they could in the evacuation hospital and then had him flown to the 300th General Hospital in Naples. Brissie had blood transfusions, bone grafts, arteries tied off, severed nerve ends taken care of. Two months later, in February, he was sent back to what the G.I.'s used to call the Z.I., the Zone of the Interior, the United States. There he went through another series of operations. The muscles in the left leg had been terribly damaged and the doctors tried to reconstruct things so that Brissie would have some strength in it. All in all, Lou had twenty-three operations on his leg and forty blood transfusions. The leg ended up nothing but bone with a few tendons and strings of muscle to make it work, but it was saved. It was shorter than the right leg now, but it was a leg.

In the summer of 1945, Lou was at Valley Forge General Hospital just outside Philadelphia. He was on crutches by now and he got a pass and went to Connie Mack Stadium, which was known then as Shibe Park, to see Connie Mack and the Athletics. Mack remembered Brissie and welcomed him. Lou asked if he could work out. Supporting himself on one leg and one crutch, he tried to pitch. People who were there said that there were tears in Connie Mack's eyes. He told Brissie to wait and get the strength back in his leg and then come back and work out. In his heart, Mack didn't think Brissie would ever be back and neither did anyone else who saw him that afternoon.

In the hospital Lou shed his crutches and made himself walk with a cane, which amazed the doctors. His leg was repeatedly put into casts, but Brissie refused to keep the casts on. He reasoned that the only way to get strength back in the withered, shattered leg was to exercise it, and he could not exercise it in a cast. So he cut the casts off and exercised, lying on his back and lifting the leg up in the air and bending it at the knee. It hurt terribly, and progress was slow.

But progress it was. After a while a brace was fitted to the leg and Brissie was able to walk pretty well without the cane. He went home to South Carolina and in the spring of 1946, less than a year and a half after he had been wounded, he tried to play some baseball around home. He overdid it. He was okay after one game but in the next he ran out of steam; he pitched awkwardly, got racked up, and hurt his arm. He wasn't able to pitch for nearly two months. But when he did start to throw again the arm felt good. He wrote to the Athletics and told them and they invited him up north. They let him pitch batting practice.

But things got bad again. His leg became infected and he had to go back into the hospital for six weeks. And then his father died. For a while during that depressing year, and for the first and only time, Lou Brissie felt like quitting.

But he didn't. Instead, after he left the hospital he did more exercises and kept throwing. He let Mack and the Athletics know that he was working, that he was getting into shape. In December of 1946 the Athletics signed him to a contract—probably because Mack admired his courage and persistence—and in the spring of 1947 he reported to the Athletics' training camp, a professional ballplayer at last.

He wore an aluminum brace on his left leg and over it he wore a shin guard which he covered with his uniform stocking. Surprisingly, he looked pretty good in spring training and the Athletics decided to hold on to him. Brissie was afraid they might be keeping him because they felt sorry for him. He was determined to make it on his own and he asked that he be sent somewhere where he would have a chance to pitch. He did not want to sit around and have people feel sorry for him.

The Athletics sent him to Savannah in the South Atlantic League, and Brissie showed them what he could do. He started slowly—he was allowed to go only four innings in his first game, even though he was pitching a shutout—but he finished like a racehorse. He won twenty-three games, lost only five, had an earned-run average of 1.90, and set a new league record for strikeouts with 273! By the tail end of that season he was a major leaguer. The Athletics called him up and he pitched one game, against the Yankees. He lost 5–3, but it didn't matter—he had made the big time. That winter the Philadelphia sports writers gave him a trophy as the most courageous athlete of the year.

But that isn't the end of the story. In the spring of 1948 he looked so good in spring training that Connie Mack made him one of his top starting pitchers, and on April 19, 1948, Brissie went against the Red Sox in Boston in one game of the annual Patriots' Day doubleheader. It was Brissie's second major league game, his first of that year, and he was going against a great-hitting Boston team that included Ted Williams, Vernon Stephens, Bobby Doerr, Dominic DiMaggio, Johnny Pesky, Birdie Tebbetts, and all the rest. Boston finished that season in a tie for the pennant, only to lose in the playoff.

Brissie pitched beautifully. He struck out seven men. But in the sixth inning Ted Williams, the most powerful hitter in baseball and usually a dead right field hitter, swung and sent a vicious line drive right back at Brissie. It smashed into his wounded leg, just below the knee, and ricocheted all the way into right field. Brissie fell to the ground, writhing with pain, and a sportswriter in the press box shook his head sadly and said, "He's all finished. He's all through. What a shame."

Players from both teams gathered around him. Williams,

who had run down to first base after his hit, hurried over to the mound. Brissie looked up at him, grinned, and said, "Good lord, Ted. Why don't you hit the ball to right field the way you're supposed to?"

He got to his feet and hobbled around for a while. He would not let them take him out. He went on pitching. In the last of the ninth, with Philadelphia leading 4–2, Ted Williams came to bat against Brissie again. Ted swung at the first pitch and fouled the ball into the left field stands. He swung at the second pitch and fouled one over the left field roof. Despite the memory of that line drive right at him, Brissie wasn't easing up on his fast ball to make sure that Williams would pull the ball safely to right. Instead he threw the ball hard, making it difficult for Williams to pull. He missed with the next pitch for ball one. Then he threw a hard curve—and Williams struck out! Brissie retired the side and won the game 4–2 for his first major league victory. He had given the powerful Red Sox only four hits, and none after Williams hit the line drive off his shin.

Brissie had to go into the hospital for observation after the game, but he came out again quickly and went on to win fourteen games for the Athletics that season and sixteen the next. His leg troubled him from time to time, but he stayed in the major leagues for six seasons, first as a starter and later as an effective relief pitcher. In the spring of 1954 he retired and became Commissioner of the American Legion Junior Baseball program. His name is not widely known any more and many younger fans probably have never heard of him, but no one who ever saw him pitch will ever forget a 6-foot 4-inch mountain of courage named Lou Brissie.

Little Man with a Big Heart

(*Chapter 14*)

One of the hardest things some boys have to face is not being big. It's something that adults usually don't understand because, big or small, we have become used to things and we know that size is not as important as, for example, hard work or determination or confidence or any number of things that are a matter of a man's character. When you are thirty or forty or fifty you sometimes forget what it can be like for a boy of thirteen or fourteen or fifteen who is inches shorter and pounds lighter than everybody else.

Even when it is only a temporary state of affairs it can bother a boy to a point of absolute discouragement. When I say temporary, I mean that some kids start to grow earlier in life than others and some a lot later. Some fellows I knew had their full growth when they were in the ninth grade; others were still fuzzy-faced boys when they graduated from high school. Ten years later on, when both were in their middle twenties, you couldn't have guessed in a million years that one of them was almost a foot taller and seventy pounds heavier than the other when both were fifteen.

I know of a boy just a few years ago who more or less threw away almost three years of his life in high school just because he was small. He had been a terrific athlete when he was smaller, a star in Little League baseball. It took a long time and a lot of effort for him to become a good ballplayer, but I guess he forgot all about that later on in high school. He had first gone out for the Little League when he was eight, just a couple of days after his birthday, as a matter of fact, and he didn't make it. He was cut. They didn't have a minor league Little League at that time in his town, so he had no team to play on. He felt bad that he didn't make it, but that didn't make him quit playing baseball. (I think maybe he had more guts at eight than he did at fourteen and fifteen, as you will see in a minute.) He played baseball every chance he could all spring and summer, and he watched every Little League game that was played.

That sort of interest is noticed. People know that someone who is that interested in something will work hard at it, and they tend to give you a break when a chance comes. The next year when Brian tried out, at the age of nine, he made the Little League. He was only the fifteenth man on his team, which meant that he didn't get to play too often. He was the reserve right fielder. But he was there, and he practiced, and he tried, and he learned. He didn't have much to give to his team at that time, except spirit and cheering, but what he had he gave. He never griped. He was always around, ready to play if they needed him, and he was always practicing, always trying, always learning. He didn't know it, but he was getting ready for his big chance.

The third year, when he was ten, he was the regular right fielder, and he played in practically every game. He still wasn't *very* good, but he was good enough to be a regular. Toward the end of the season, the manager stuck him in at shortstop once in a while for an inning or so, just to give him experience. In the last game of the season, he was at shortstop in the last inning, when all of a sudden the game got tied up and went into extra innings, and here was the right fielder playing shortstop.

His father was watching the game and he was nervous. He told me, "I didn't realize how much time Brian had put in practicing at short. I though he didn't know what to do." The boy's team got a run in the top of the eighth (in case anyone reading this has been out of the country for the last fifteen years and has never seen a Little League game and is wondering how come the eighth inning is an extra inning, I'd better explain that in Little League ball six innings is an official game). But then, in the bottom of the eighth, the other team got the tying and winning runs on second and third with only one out.

Brian's father told me, "I was praying. I was saying, 'Please, don't let them hit it to Brian.' I was thinking, here he was at a strange position in a key moment in a crucial game. I was scared that he'd fumble the ball if it was hit to him, and two runs would come in, and the team would lose, and he'd feel terrible."

Well, the batter did hit it to Brian, and on the first pitch. It was a hard bouncer and Brian was playing up close to cut the run off at the plate. He fielded the ball cleanly and threw it to the catcher who tagged the man coming in from third. Then the catcher wheeled and threw to first and the batter, who must have been slower than a turtle, was out! It was a double play, Brian to the catcher to first, and the game was over. They had won. Brian was a hero.

The next year Brian was the regular shortstop from the beginning of the season. He was only eleven and only average size, but that was his position. He got his hits, he played good ball, and he made the league's all-star team that went into the district elimination tournament. They got beaten 1–0 in the first game they played, when a big kid, big for twelve, shut them out with two hits. But as a ballplayer I'm impressed by the fact that Brian got one of the two hits. I mean, he was not scared of standing up at the plate against the great big pitcher the other team had. He hung in there, he swung his bat, and he got a hit.

In his last year in the Little League, when he was twelve, he played shortstop and he pitched. He was a star by now, though he still wasn't very big. You know how some Little League teams depend on one boy who has gotten real big real early. But Brian was just a twelve-year-old boy who happened to be a good athlete who had worked hard at learning the game. He knew what to do. He not only played Little League ball two nights a week, he played on his class team in school and he played on a neighborhood team that played games on Saturdays. He played a *lot* of baseball. At the end of that Little League season he was named to the all-star team again and this time he was elected captain of the team. The team got eliminated early again in the district eliminations, but Brian played his usual good game.

The next year, when he was in the seventh grade, he was ineligible for Little League because you can play the year you are thirteen only if your birthday comes after

August 1, and Brian's birthday was in the spring. So, at the ripe old age of thirteen he was a retired ballplayer. He still played on his class team and on the neighborhood team, but he was marking time, waiting to go out for the high school team when he reached the ninth grade. He didn't try for the Pony League, which is the next League above Little League, because some of the guys looked pretty big and he felt too small. He just didn't want to try.

By the time he was in the eighth grade he didn't only feel small, he was small. He was one of those people who get their growth late. He had been an average size boy in the sixth grade, but in the eighth he was one of the littlest kids in his class.

By the time he reached ninth grade—when he could go out for baseball—he was miserable. He had hardly any friends. One of his closest pals when they were both playing Little League ball had sprouted early and was now almost six feet tall. Brian was about five feet two.

It was tough. It was unfair, too, though there wasn't much anyone could do about it. But the bad thing about it was—Brian quit. He wouldn't go out for baseball, or any sport, because he was too small. He *knew* he wasn't good enough, so he didn't try. He forgot about himself at the age of eight, trying anyway even though there wasn't any chance. He just quit. He didn't play any sports, and he didn't watch any sports. He said he didn't like sports any more. What he meant was, he didn't think he was good enough but he didn't want anybody to find out.

If he had spent his time studying or in some other school activity, it wouldn't have been so bad. But he moped around and neglected his books, and didn't join any activities. He didn't do anything but feel sorry for himself.

He moped for almost three years. In his junior year he finally started to grow, and by the time he was a senior he was close to six feet tall himself. Then he decided to go out for baseball—and made the team. But he wasn't much. He spent most of the time on the bench. He had forgotten an awful lot about baseball, and hadn't learned anything new. Baseball stays pretty much the same, but little things change and good players know what they are and use them to advantage. Brian was at a disadvantage. All his skills were rusty, and even though he had the size he wasn't half the ballplayer he had been when he was small. He hadn't played, practiced, or learned. I guess his idea through those years of doing nothing was, if he couldn't be a star the way he was in Little League, then the heck with it. All he did was waste almost three years, when he could have been learning how while he waited for his body to catch up to what he was learning.

Brian is a nice boy. He is in college now, and his grades are good, and he'll be a fine man. But he doesn't have the confidence he should have. I keep thinking, if only he hadn't quit on himself when he was slow growing up he would have had a lot happier time in high school and he'd be a lot happier now.

The point is: you can't quit because you're too small or too skinny or too fat. You can't worry about people laughing at you. There will always be stupid people who laugh at somebody else having trouble. But don't ever think you are the first one or the only one who has been laughed at, or hooted at, or booed. Don't quit. Keep trying. Look, I am a major league ballplayer and that's a pretty good thing to be. It means that I am one of the five hundred best baseball players in a country of 191,000,000 people. But I get booed (oh, boy, do I get booed sometimes). Roger Maris hit sixty-one home runs and he got booed and hooted at. Ted Williams got booed. Even Willie Mays, whom everybody admires, gets criticized now and then.

When you are criticized, you're in good company. If you quit because you are being criticized or because you think you will be, and that people are going to laugh at you or sneer at you or poke fun at you if you don't make it, then you're in bad company—you're a quitter. All you do when you quit is prove that you're not going to make it. You don't even give yourself a chance. It's like going up to the plate and saying, "I have three strikes on me," and walking away without even trying to swing a bat. If you swing, at least you have a chance of hitting the ball. If you try, at anything, you have a better chance than if you don't try. If you keep on trying, you have a better chance than if you don't keep on trying.

When I came up to the Yankees there was a little fellow on our club who never should have been in the major leagues. I'm not quite six feet tall but I towered over this man. He was only five feet six. There are quite a few high school kids around who are five feet six who are moaning about being too small. But this man was thirty-two years old and he was playing major league baseball. And not only playing it, he was playing it better than anybody else around. The season before he had been named the Most Valuable Player in the American League. He was the most valuable player on the Yankee team that won the league pennant and then took the World Series in four straight games. And he was only five feet six inches tall.

His name, of course, was Phil Rizzuto. Phil is not the only little fellow to make it to the majors. There was Bobby Shantz, who is five feet six and a quarter and weighs 138 pounds. He won the Most Valuable Player award two years after Phil did. That means that in two out of three seasons fellows who were short even by high school standards were the best ballplayers in the American League. Albie Pearson, a .300-hitting outfielder, is even shorter than Phil and Bobby. Albie is only five feet four. And there have been quite a few others. I guess they all must have had to fight as hard as Phil Rizzuto did to make it. But I knew Phil best, so I'll tell you about him.

When Phil was about seventeen or eighteen he had played a lot of good sandlot baseball around New York City and, like other New York kids, he went to the tryouts that were held each year by the Yankees, Giants, and Dodgers. The big league coaches and scouts who ran the tryouts thought he was kidding. They thought he was a showoff who turned up just for laughs. When they found out that he was serious, they told him he was too small and to go on home. They weren't being cruel. They were being practical. Baseball is, by and large, a big man's game. In 1964 about 75 per cent of the players listed on big league rosters were at least six feet tall.

Here was little Phil in a forest of big, rangy kids. And he had been told by big league scouts that he was too little, that he didn't have a chance. My friend Brian knew that he didn't have a chance to play high school baseball because he was too small, so he didn't even try. But Phil knew that if he didn't even try, if he quit when he was told to quit, he would never play big league ball, he would never even have a chance. So he didn't quit. He kept coming around, like a fly buzzing around a kitchen door on a summer's day, and finally somebody opened the door a little and Phil had his chance.

He *was* too small, and he always would be. He wasn't strong enough. His arm never really was as good as it should have been. He was too little to hit overpowering big league pitching. He never should have made it in the minors, let alone the majors. But he did. He signed a contract and he played four years of minor league ball. He batted .310, .336, .316, and .347, and in that last year he was named the best minor league ballplayer in the country by *The Sporting News*, the baseball newspaper. He came up to the Yankees and in his first year batted .307. In 1950 he hit .324, and was named the Most Valuable Player in the league. Phil was a major leaguer for sixteen years, counting the three years he was in the Navy during World War II. He was on nine pennant winners, on seven World Series winners, and was named to the American League All-Star team five times. How many six-footers can say that?

You can't quit. Even when everyone else had told Rizzuto that he would never make it—when even the major league scouts, men who knew their business and who were looking for good ballplayers, had told him—Phil didn't give up. He kept playing and practicing and learning and developing his skills and polishing them and shining them up and getting them ready and working on them, waiting for the day—the day somebody opened that door for him.

When the door opened, Phil didn't have to *start* to learn. He was ready.

Those years of preparation paid off for him all through his career. There was one play in particular that is talked about by people who saw it the way writers talk about Shakespeare. It was so perfect. The Yankees were playing the Cleveland Indians late in the season, and it was a big game, one that would have a lot to say about who would win the pennant that year. Joe DiMaggio was on third base and Rizzuto was up. The Cleveland third baseman looked at Rizzuto and then at DiMaggio.

"I wonder if Phil is going to bunt," he said.

DiMaggio had already gotten the sign for the squeeze play but he said, "No, he's not going to bunt."

But the Indian third baseman was watching closely, ready for the bunt possibility. Even so, the Yankees went through with the squeeze. DiMaggio broke for home with the windup. The pitcher fired the ball and little Phil, as calm as a man reaching out to knock on a door, tapped the prettiest squeeze bunt you ever saw down the third base line. The third baseman didn't have a chance. DiMaggio scored standing up on Rizzuto's bunt, and the Yankees won the game and went on to win the pennant.

It was a perfect play, a perfect bunt. I wonder how many times Phil practiced dropping squeeze bunts when he was playing on the sandlots, when he was getting himself ready for the chance that everyone told him would never come.

You can't quit. That's all there is to it. You can't decide ahead of time that you're not good enough.

Ask Phil Rizzuto.

Biggest Comeback Ever

(Chapter 15)

I've had troubles at times in my major league career—I've had operations on both knees, I've pulled muscles in my thighs, I've broken my foot, once I hurt my shoulder so badly that I had trouble throwing—and I've really worried about these things. But I'll tell you the truth, your own worries seem like nothing when you think of the things that other people have been bothered with. When I compare the troubles I've had in baseball with what Jimmy Piersall went through, I get sort of ashamed to even mention mine. His story is one of the strangest and most courageous in baseball history.

Jimmy Piersall had a difficult boyhood. He had a brother almost twenty years older than he was who got married when Jimmy was still a baby and who died before Jimmy ever really knew him. So Jimmy was brought up as an only child. His father had been an orphan who had lived in foster homes and institutions and who had to fight for everything he ever got. He loved Jimmy as any father would love his son, but he was harsh and strict and demanding. Jimmy grew up worrying constantly about what his father would think of almost everything he did, whether he would approve or disapprove. Everybody feels that way to a certain extent—and it's right and proper that they should—but in the Piersall home in Jimmy's case it was carried to an extreme. Jimmy grew up to be a worrier about everything, and particularly about himself and whether he was doing well enough.

The Piersalls were poor. Jim's father was a house painter. When there was work the Piersalls lived well enough, but there wasn't much work. Jim grew up during the 1930s when the Depression was on in this country, and not many people could spare money to have their house painted. The Piersalls had a hard time and they all lived under a strain. It's hard to keep serene and contented when there isn't money enough to buy the things you need. Eventually, it got to Jimmy's mother and she had a nervous breakdown when Jimmy was about seven years old. For ten years she was in and out of hospitals. She would come home, apparently all right, but then she would get sick again. Once, when she was upset, she left the house and walked across a busy street filled with traffic, apparently not even noticing it, and Jimmy, who was only eight years old, had to run out and grab her to keep her from being killed.

It was a hard life for a small boy. Jimmy wrote in his book, *Fear Strikes Out*, "During that time, I had never known a moment when I didn't worry about her. When she was away, I worried how long she'd be gone. When she was home, I worried how long it would be before she would have to go away again. Each day she was with us, I left the house with the gnawing fear that she might not be there when I got home. I was afraid to go to school, and afraid to walk into the house after I got home."

Like most fathers, Jimmy's father wanted him to be a

baseball player, a major leaguer. From the time Jim was just a little boy his father worked with him, throwing baseballs to him, telling him what to do and what not to do. Because his father's approval was the most important thing in Jimmy's life, and his disapproval the worst thing that could happen, Jimmy worried constantly about baseball, too, worrying whether he'd be good enough.

His father never wanted him to play football, for fear he'd injure himself and ruin his chances in baseball. One day, when Jim had a chance to play in a junior varsity game, and did, and starred in it (he intercepted a pass behind his own goal line and ran more than a hundred yards for a touchdown), he was afraid to tell his father about it. And another time, when he broke his wrist playing touch football, he worried more about his father finding out about it than the fact that his wrist was hurt.

Tension built up constantly inside Piersall, and as a high school kid he was a bundle of nerves. He did everything at full speed. When he was fifteen he woke up one morning with a terrible headache. It eased off after a while, but from that time on he woke up every morning with that same headache. It would go away somewhat during the day, but it was always there. It stayed with him for seven years, until he was hospitalized when he was twenty-two years old.

Meanwhile, he developed into a superb baseball player. After he graduated from high school he was offered a twenty-thousand-dollar bonus from the Braves, who were then still in Boston. He also had offers from the Detroit Tigers, the Yankees, and the Dodgers. But his father wanted him to skip the bonus and sign with the Boston

Red Sox. At that time, a "bonus" player had to stay on the roster of the major league team that signed him, and Mr. Piersall wanted Jimmy to have the advantage of playing minor league ball for a few seasons. The Red Sox worked out a deal that pleased the Piersalls, and Jimmy signed.

Piersall was sent to Scranton in the Eastern League, where he batted .281 and led the league in runs batted in and putouts. More important, he met the girl who was to become his wife. They were married at the end of the following season, which he spent at Louisville in the American Association. The next season Jimmy was with Louisville again, and at the end of that year the Red Sox called him up to the majors. No one knew it at the time, but for the tense, excitable, constantly worrying Piersall, the bad time of his life had already begun. His wife had been very ill that year. She got better and left the hospital, but then had a relapse and almost died. After a series of blood transfusions she regained her strength and perfect good health, but it had been a long siege. The Louisville club insisted that he take time off and stay with his wife when she was so ill, and Jimmy did. But between worrying about Mary and worrying about his job with the ball club, and worrying about his baseball future, the already tense Piersall got more jittery than ever.

The next spring the Red Sox kept him with the parent club all through training and brought him to Boston for Opening Day. Jimmy, a rookie, rode the bench for the first few games of the season. He couldn't stand the inaction and asked the Red Sox to send him to the minors so that he could play every day. The Red Sox agreed and sent him back to Louisville again. It didn't work out. As Jim said later, "I was a scared, tense kid who had just been through a series of shattering experiences. I made Higgins [the new Louisville manager] nervous with my perpetual moving around, my constant yelling, my everlasting restlessness."

After only seventeen games Piersall was benched, though he was hitting over .300. He became depressed and jumpy. He worried about money. He worried about losing his job in baseball. He and Mary had had their first baby that spring, and Jim was also supporting his mother and his father, who now had a heart condition and could not work at all. Jim began to do irrational things. On a road trip he phoned his wife and told her to drive up from home with the baby and meet him. Then he learned that he had been sent down to Birmingham in the Southern Association. When his wife arrived, Jimmy was waiting on the sidewalk. He got in the car, turned it around, drove back to Louisville and then on to Birmingham, doing all the driving himself because, he said, he was afraid that she wouldn't drive fast enough. He reached Birmingham just before a night game, put on his uniform, pinch-hit, and hit safely.

He played like a wild man all summer, and he had a great season. He batted .346 and fielded sensationally. He seemed sure to stick with Boston the next year. But that winter the old tensions came back, more strongly than ever. He still had his terrible headaches. He couldn't find an off-season job. He worried about money. He felt the financial drain of supporting four people other than himself (his wife, his baby, his father, his mother). Mary was expecting another child.

Then one day he read by chance that the Red Sox were planning to convert him from the outfield to shortstop the next year. It was the first he had heard about it, and it shook him up. He became convinced that the Red Sox didn't want him or need him, and this was all part of a plan to get rid of him.

All Jimmy's torments and worries twisted about this one idea. He was barely twenty-two years old, married, with one child and expecting another. He was the sole support of two ill and aging parents. And he was suddenly positive that he was all washed up as a baseball player. The tensions and terrors that had nagged him all his life boiled over. He slowly went out of his mind with worry. He spent the rest of the winter hiding in movies and fretting about what he would do in spring training, and when he finally went south he slyly refused to take his baseball glove with him. That was his escape. He figured out irrationally that when the Red Sox found he didn't have a glove he would be able to come right back home again.

He arrived in Florida, took a cab to the hotel the Boston team was staying at, paid the cabdriver, picked up his bag, went into the hotel—and that's all Jimmy Piersall remembers about that season until August, when he woke up in the violent ward of a sanitarium.

That was the year that Piersall *was* switched to shortstop, and successfully, at least at first. He made the big leagues and in a strange position. On Opening Day he was playing shortstop and batting sixth. But he began

117

to act oddly. He clowned constantly. He mocked fellow players. He delayed games while he fooled around. He got into fistfights with rival players and with his own teammates. He argued beyond all reason with umpires. He was so restless that he couldn't stay still for an instant.

The Red Sox thought he might calm down if they switched him back to the outfield, but it didn't do much good. They let him sit on the bench for a while, but there Piersall was worse than ever. He couldn't sit still. He bothered everybody. One day he was listed in the starting lineup, but a last-minute change of plans put him on the bench again. Jimmy was so upset that he burst into tears and cried for almost fifteen minutes, right there in the dugout where everyone, players, writers, fans, could see him.

Everybody who knew him was worried. He was antagonizing his teammates, his opponents, the umpires, everybody. Finally, the Red Sox decided that Piersall might snap out of his odd, edgy, high-strung mood if he were sent back down to Birmingham for a while. And Jimmy told his wife that he would reform, that he would settle down. But at Birmingham he was worse than ever. He was there only twenty days but in that time he was thrown out of six games, was suspended four times, and twice flew back to Boston on impulse.

The second time he went back to Boston he was persuaded by the Red Sox to go to a sanitarium for treatment. He reluctantly agreed, but twice within a few days he walked out of the place. He went back but one day he went berserk, fought with the attendants, and was put in the violent ward.

In the hospital Jimmy received the best treatment possible. He was in bad shape for only a few weeks, and then suddenly one day in August he was okay. For the first time in more than seven years, he had no headache. He had no memory of all the bad things that had happened since the first day of spring training. But he was able to talk about everything and to realize what had happened to him. He had to take it slow and easy for several months as he regained his poise and confidence. But the main thing was, he was cured.

Coming back in baseball was still ahead of him, though. There is tremendous pressure on everybody. Could a man who had been through what Piersall had been through stand up to that pressure? The proof of that is in what Jimmy accomplished that next year, and in the years that followed. By nature Piersall is a lively, bouncy man, and fans who have seen him since his recovery know that he is one of the most volatile and excitable—as well as exciting—players in the game. But the doctors told him not to worry about that. They told him it was important that he not keep everything suppressed inside himself, that he should not let his worries and resentments build up. They told him to relax, enjoy things, sound off when something bothered him. And Jimmy did. And it worked beautifully. Even when an unthinking fan yelled a cruel and stupid thing like, "You screwball, you ought to be in an asylum," all Piersall did was grin up at the stands and yell back, "Don't you wish you were making as much money as this screwball is?" He didn't let those little things bother him.

But that first year back was awfully hard. Jimmy knew

that everyone would be watching him, wondering about him. Some people said things that hurt his feelings badly. Others tried too hard to avoid talking about his trouble. And all through this, Jimmy was trying to regain a place in major league baseball.

I know that big league ball can be tense and nerve-wracking for anybody. For a man who had gone through what Jimmy had, it must have been unbearable at times. There had to be times when Piersall wanted to quit, get out of the pressure cooker, and go find a nice quiet job behind a desk someplace. But he didn't. He made himself go through with it. He said later that coming back was made easier for him because of the way everyone in baseball treated him. But I keep thinking of the things yelled at him from the stands—and sometimes from the dugouts in the heat of a close game. I keep remembering that along with getting back into circulation again, along with meeting people all over again and proving that he was all right, along with getting used to the fact that some people would always be a bit suspicious of him, Jimmy Piersall had to prove himself as a ballplayer. He had to make it as a major leaguer.

Well, he did it. He proved himself. He played 151 games for the Red Sox the first year he came back and he batted .272, which is pretty good for a man in what really was his rookie year in the big leagues. He tied a major league record in June by getting six hits in six at bats in one game. He led the league in sacrifice hits. He led all the outfielders in double plays that season.

More than that, he made some of the greatest catches any outfielder ever made anywhere. I remember one he made off me. The day before he had robbed the Yankees of a victory by turning a home run into an out with a great catch. This day I was batting righthanded and I pushed a ball deep to right center in Fenway Park, way back toward the bullpen. I thought it was a homer or, if it didn't reach the fence, a sure triple. But Piersall went over and back to the bullpen fence, jumped, balanced himself on his right hand and at the same time reached up with his glove hand and caught the ball. I kicked about a ton of dirt out of that infield, and up in the press box one of the New York sportswriters wrote, "In 27 years of covering baseball, I never saw a catch like it."

He made plays like that all year long—and all through his career. I haven't seen Willie Mays in too many ball games because he's in the other league, but if Willie is a better outfielder than Piersall he must be just about the greatest ever.

When that season was over, Jimmy Piersall was named the outstanding Red Sox player of the year. He made the American League All-Star team in 1954 and again in 1956, and in 1961, toward the latter part of his career, he batted .322 for Cleveland. He came back from a disaster to become a top-flight major leaguer for more than ten seasons. There is no question that along with being one of the best fielders and one of the most colorful players that I ever saw, Jimmy Piersall has got to be one of the most courageous. The title of his book, *Fear Strikes Out,* sums it up. When Jimmy was young he was strangled by fear, but he ended up by defeating fear, by striking it out of his life.

Fat Freddie's Fight

(*Chapter 16*)

Fred Fitzsimmons was a major league pitcher for almost twenty years and later on he was a manager, briefly, with the Philadelphia Phillies, and a coach with several teams. Off the field he was kind and pleasant, a very friendly and likable man. On the field he was tough, a tremendous competitor, one of the hardest fighters for his side that you ever saw.

The oddest thing about Fitzsimmons' record is the fact that he started four World Series games, lost three, and never won one. You will occasionally hear people who should know better saying things like this ballplayer is no good in the clutch and that that ballplayer always loses the big games. They said that about Don Newcombe of the Brooklyn Dodgers when he couldn't beat the Yankees in 1955 and 1956 in the World Series. They forgot two things. One was that Newcombe was a fast ball pitcher; he was very strong and threw hard but he seldom threw a curve and when he did it wasn't a really good curve. The Yankees were fast ball hitters, the best fast ball-hitting team in baseball. The second thing was that Newcombe won forty-seven games in the National League in those two seasons, and a lot of those were very big games; if he hadn't won them the Dodgers would not have won the pennant. We didn't beat him because he "couldn't win the big games." We beat him because we could hit fast ball pitchers. And even at that, it wasn't easy with Newcombe. I want to get back to Freddie Fitzsimmons, but there is one more point about Newcombe. In the seventh game of the 1956 Series, Yogi Berra knocked two home runs and practically beat Newcombe singlehanded. That's when everyone said Newcombe didn't have it when it counted. But I remember that last game. I had one of my best seasons that year, and had been hitting well in the Series, but early in the game, with a man on base and one out, Newcombe struck me out. Then he struck Berra out, too, except that Yogi tipped the ball and catcher Roy Campanella dropped the tip to give Yogi a life. And then Yogi hit the first of his two homers. If Roy had been lucky enough to hold on to that foul tip, Newk would have been out of the inning and that seventh game might have been different.

Anyway, I mention all this to show how a man can get a bad rap, get a bad reputation for something he doesn't deserve. Fred Fitzsimmons started four World Series games and didn't win one, and yet he was one of the most courageous pitchers of all time and one of the best competitors. He lost his first game in 1933 when he was with the New York Giants and Earl Whitehill of the Washington Senators shut the Giants out. He lost to the Yankees twice in 1936, but he had bad luck in the first game and, anyway, the Yankees hardly ever lost a World Series game in those days. And between 1927 and 1939 the Yankees, in seven Series, won twenty-eight games and lost three, and two of those defeats were to the great Carl Hubbell.

In 1941, when Fitz was with the Brooklyn Dodgers and forty years old, he was locked in a 0–0 duel against the Yanks in the seventh inning of the third game when a line drive hit him on the knee; he had to leave the game and the Yankees got to the relief pitcher and won 2–1.

Four starts, no wins. But not no courage. Sometimes courage doesn't produce obvious results. The brave man doesn't always win. But that doesn't mean he isn't brave.

Fat Freddie (he got his nickname because he was on the pudgy side) won more than two hundred games in the major leagues, but one stands out more than all the others. It came very near the end of his long career when he was playing for the Dodgers, who were managed then by Leo Durocher. As I said before, Fitz was a very nice fellow off the field but a tough man on it. He felt that he could beat certain clubs because he made them remember that he had beaten them before. He once said, "I could hear them say, 'That so-and-so again. We can't beat him.' That was just the mood I wanted to get them in. As long as they thought they couldn't beat me, and kept worrying about it, why they just weren't going to beat me. You see, there are some ballplayers around with all the ability they'll ever need to make good. But they don't think they'll ever be as good as they should be. They decide that they can't get the ball over the plate or that they can't hit the curve. So they never get anywhere. A couple of pitchers on this team were talking about Ted Williams and Stan Musial, and one of them, a guy who should have been a great pitcher except that he just never really made it, said he'd rather pitch to Williams. He was asked why and he said, 'Well, I've never pitched to Williams. Maybe I couldn't get him out, but maybe I could. I don't know. But with Musial I have no doubts. I've pitched to him and I know I can't get him out.' Well, you know, if that's the way the guy feels about it, he'll *never* get Musial out. You can beat people by convincing them that you're better than they are."

The Fitzsimmons game to remember took place late in the 1941 season. The year before at the age of thirty-nine Fred had set a National League record for won-and-lost percentage when he won sixteen games and lost only two. In 1941 he won six and lost one. In other words, over a two-season stretch at the age when most old pitchers (except Warren Spahn) are washed up, Fitz won twenty-two games and lost three. What is extra-special about this is the fact that in five previous seasons he had lost forty-two games while winning only thirty-eight. He had been a losing pitcher. Then he got proud and with a good Dodger team around him finished his career in a blaze of glory. He did it with competitive toughness, courage in the clutch, as he showed in this game late in 1941.

The Dodgers were playing the St. Louis Cardinals in a crucial series in St. Louis. Brooklyn's pitching staff was working overtime and Leo Durocher decided to gamble with old Freddie in the opening game of the series. He rested him for almost two weeks and then threw him against the Cards.

The game went eleven innings. Fitzsimmons puffed and struggled, inning by inning, hanging on, just grunting when Durocher would ask him if he could go one more inning. He was really fighting.

The key moment came late in the game when the Cardinals loaded the bases with two outs and had Johnny

Mize at the plate. Mize was a great hitter, one of the very best of all time. More than that, he was a lefthanded hitter and Fitzsimmons was a righthanded pitcher. Durocher wondered whether he should take Fitz out, but Fitzsimmons was positive that he could take care of Mize.

Leo loves to talk about what happened. Fitzsimmons bullied Mize, who was much bigger and much younger. He threatened to hit him with a pitch, which he certainly wouldn't have done in a spot like that and force in a run, but he threw the ball very tight and Mize ducked into the dirt. Fitzsimmons got a strike across and then yelled at Mize that he was going to go down again. Mize had to jump out of the way of another pitch.

Durocher says he ran out to talk to Freddie, warning him not to hit Mize because it would force in that run, but he says that Fitzsimmons wasn't even listening to him. He got strike two across and again he yelled and bullied Mize. John, as nice a man as he is big, didn't say a word, but he had to duck again. Now the count was three and two, and everything had come down to the wire. Fitzsimmons was still raging at Mize, and he yelled that the next pitch was going to be a fast ball right down the middle. He defied Mize to hit it.

According to Leo, Fitzsimmons always grunted when he threw his fast ball. This time he wound up, turned toward the plate, grunted—and threw up the slowest, prettiest, change-up curve you ever saw. Mize, expecting the fast ball, was so surprised that he took it for strike three. Fitzsimmons walked off the field as though it were nothing. He wasn't as good a pitcher as Mize was a hitter, but that day he wanted to win so badly that he convinced himself he could. He convinced himself that he could get Mize out. And he was right. I sure don't recommend throwing at people, though I think it's pretty obvious that Freddie Fitzsimmons was not throwing *at* John Mize. What he was doing was defeating him, and in defeating Mize he was winning a big game for the Dodgers. Freddie was convinced he would win. What he had, the quality inside him that made him win, was the courage of his convictions.

You see that same feeling in all great athletes and, probably, in all great men, the belief that you can do anything if that's what you have to do. No great athlete ever assumed ahead of time that he was going to do anything else but win. And no great man ever assumed that he was going to be anything but a success.

Campy

(*Chapter 17*)

I have played in more than ten World Series and a lot of great things have happened in them, but one moment I remember particularly had to do with something—and someone—who wasn't even on the ball field.

It was in 1958. We had lost the first two games of the Series to the Braves in Milwaukee and now we were back in Yankee Stadium for the third game. I was in center field in the top of the second inning when, apparently for no reason, a cheer started in the stands and grew and got bigger and louder until it seemed that every one of the 71,599 people in Yankee Stadium were standing and applauding. It took a minute or so to figure out what was happening. Then it became obvious.

Roy Campanella had come into the ball park.

Campy had been seriously injured in an automobile accident the previous January, when the car he was driving to his home on Long Island skidded and bounced off a pole. The car was smashed, and Campanella ended up in a heap on the floor of the car. His neck was broken. After the police got him out of the car and an ambulance had taken him to the hospital, the doctors found out that he was paralyzed from the neck down.

It was hard to believe. Campanella had played ten years

in the major leagues, and had won the Most Valuable Player award in the National League three times, in 1951, 1953, and 1955. In 1953, in what was probably the best of all his good seasons, he batted .312, hit forty-two home runs (still the most ever hit by a major league catcher in one season), scored 103 runs, and batted in 142 runs. Over his ten-year career, he *averaged* twenty-four home runs and eighty-five runs batted in per season. He was a great handler of pitchers, too, and he had a strong arm. Even though he was a Dodger and tried to beat the Yankees in five different World Series, I have to admit that he was a wonderful ballplayer.

But more than that, he was a bouncy, lively man, always talking, laughing, telling jokes, moving around, kidding, doing things. He enjoyed being alive. He never got conceited or too good for anybody when he became famous. He was always pleasant and friendly, a really natural man.

I've been told a couple of stories that show this part of Campy's personality—the fact that he was a naturally nice guy. Both happened in Vero Beach, Florida, where the Dodgers train in the spring.

A sportswriter was looking for Campy one evening to ask him a few questions. Now, the Dodger camp is different from most big league training camps in that everybody lives right on the training grounds in a sort of army barracks arrangement. It's a lot fancier than an army barracks, but the kitchen and the dining room and the recreation rooms and the sleeping quarters are all part of the Dodger camp itself, where in other camps, like the Yankees', the players live in a hotel or a motel and eat in regular restaurants and go out to the ball park in the morning. I don't know which way is better. I like the way the Yankees do it, but that may be because I'm used to it.

Anyway, the Dodgers have one great big camp, with everything on it, including the kitchen. The writer was looking for Campy and asked the Dodger publicity man if he knew where Roy was. The publicity man grinned. He told the writer to follow him, and led him around to the back of the dining hall to where the kitchen was. Outside the kitchen door, squeezing oranges for juice for the morning, were several of the people who worked in the kitchen, and Campanella. They were shooting the breeze, talking about this thing and that, having a pleasant time while they worked. Campanella was working right along with the others, helping them out for the fun of it and because he was enjoying himself. The Dodger publicity man said to the writer, "We have the highest-paid orange juice squeezer in the world."

Another day, the Dodgers were playing an intrasquad game before the regular exhibition schedule began. The club was split into two squads, most of them rookies. Regular players who had finished working out were taking showers and getting dressed. But Campanella came over to watch the game, and after a couple of minutes he started taking care of the bats that were lying around near the bench. He stacked them neatly and began to act as the bat boy. He gave each player his bat as he went up to the plate, retrieved it after the man had hit, and put it back with the others. He knelt in the on-deck circle with the next batter.

The regular bat boy for the Dodgers, a fellow named

Charlie DiGiovanni, who died only a few years later, had been helping out in the clubhouse when the game began, but came over to the field in about the second inning. When he saw Campy doing his job, he smiled but didn't say anything. He sat on the bench behind Campy and watched for a while. After an inning or so, Campanella happened to look around and he saw Charlie. He grinned and said, "How am I doing, Charlie?" DiGiovanni, who had a pretty good sense of humor, shook his head sadly and said, "You'll never make it, kid."

Campy laughed and kept on being bat boy. The Dodger publicity man said, "We also have the highest-paid bat boy in baseball."

But both those things were typical of Roy. He was a cheerful, pleasant, active, busy man, always doing something. I guess that was the reason, as much as the fact that he was such a great ballplayer, that people were so shocked when they heard of his accident. It just didn't seem possible that anyone as high-spirited as Campy could be paralyzed. I guess a lot of us thought that being made helpless would bother Roy more than it would a quieter man.

It didn't work out that way. Campy shook off despair and went to work on himself. He had to lie on a special bed on his stomach for a long time, and then he had to go through a lengthy rehabilitation program to teach his once-powerful muscles how to work all over again. The accident had damaged his nervous system, and he had little or no control over the nerves that operated the muscles of his arms and legs. He had to undergo special exercises to retrain certain muscles so that he could move his head and lift his arms. It took hours and hours of tiresome repetition of exercises before he could do the simplest things. It seemed strange to read that a man who had hit 242 home runs in the major leagues had to practice over and over again to learn how to lift a spoon from a dish to his mouth. Yet, when he did he was prouder of himself than he was when he had hit all those home runs.

He fought his way back from helplessness. He was still in the rehabilitation hospital in October, more than eight months after the operation, when Dan Topping of the Yankees invited him to the Stadium to see a World Series game between the Yanks and Braves. It was Campy's first public appearance since his accident. He was brought into the Stadium in his wheelchair, but when they found that the chair wouldn't fit down the narrow aisle leading to his box seat, the special policemen with him lifted him and carried him down to his seat. Later on, Campy said, "If I had known that they were going to have to carry me, maybe I wouldn't have gone to the game. It hurt me that I had to be seen the way I was."

But then he heard the applause. I think it must have been the biggest and loudest applause—and it sure was the most admiring applause—that Campanella or any ballplayer ever received. This time the fans weren't cheering him for one play, one home run, one run batted in, one baserunner cut down stealing. They were cheering eight long months of struggle, and they were cheering his courage in coming to the game. They knew what Campy had overcome to get that far—far enough to be in a position to be carried to a box seat.

I thought about that day five years later, in 1963, the

day before the World Series began between the Yankees and the Los Angeles Dodgers. That was a workout day for the two clubs, and the only people in Yankee Stadium were the Dodger players and the Yankee players, some sportswriters, a few photographers, and that was about all. Except that Campy was there, too. This time he was wheeled down to a box out along the right field line, and a lot of Dodger and Yankee players wandered out to visit with him. They may have come out to see him to be polite, but they stayed around chatting with him because it was fun.

He looked fine. He had gained a surprising amount of control of his arms, and he seemed very natural and relaxed. He sat there kidding and joking with us, and I think everybody forgot that he was in a wheelchair. It was like old times, and he was a natural part of it.

I remember that somebody was talking about the way baseball uniforms have changed in design in recent years, and that nowadays they were cut more like football pants, close to the leg. "They're different from the old uniforms," somebody said. "They're streamlined. The old ones used to flap in the breeze when you ran." Campanella said, "*That* was my trouble. I was wondering what it was. *That's* why I ran so slow. Those old pants slowed me down."

Everybody roared laughing, and for a moment everybody forgot that Roy Campanella couldn't run anyplace anymore. Or even walk. Campy had made everybody laugh and relax, just the way he used to.

He didn't have the same body. But he had the same courage. Campy had really come back.

Joe D. and Ted W.

(Chapter 18)

Two of the best ballplayers of all time were Joe DiMaggio and Ted Williams. They were so good and they made it look so easy—Joe at bat or in the field or on the bases, and Ted especially at bat—that there is a tendency to think that everything came easy for them. But sometimes it seems that things are actually even harder and more difficult for the really outstanding. (Take President Franklin D. Roosevelt, for example. Some people I was with recently were talking about him and one of them said what an amazing thing it was for a man who was a hopeless cripple, who couldn't walk by himself and who needed steel braces on his legs even to stand up, to become President of the greatest country in the world. One of the others there said, in surprise, "I didn't realize he was that badly crippled." Which makes it more amazing—that a man could overcome a physical handicap like that to such a point that people forget or never realized he was handicapped.)

In a way, in the field of sport, the same sort of thing applies to DiMaggio and Williams. Looking back at the great records they made, you find yourself surprised to discover or remember the handicaps they had to overcome. DiMaggio hurt his knee so badly in the minor leagues when he was playing with the San Francisco Seals that it was thought his career was over. When he returned and started playing again, the major leagues had no interest in him for a time. In all, he played four straight seasons in the Pacific Coast League before the Yankees bought him (for only twenty-five thousand dollars). And a lot of people thought the Yankees were throwing their money away.

In his first spring training with the Yankees, Joe was badly burned on the foot by a heat lamp and missed the first weeks of the season, but he came back to hit .323 and prove that his knee was all right and that he was a bona fide major leaguer. The next year he hit forty-six home runs. Two years later he led the American League in batting, and he repeated the next year. In 1941, the season that Williams hit .406 to take the batting championship away from DiMaggio, Joe had his greatest year. He overshadowed even Williams by leading the Yankees to a pennant and the world championship, by winning the Most Valuable Player award, and by setting one of the most remarkable records in baseball—batting safely in fifty-six consecutive games.

I honestly don't know how he stood up under the pressure of that hitting streak. After about thirty games, when he started closing in on the records, old and new, for batting streaks, everybody in the country must have known about DiMaggio. They even wrote a song about him that went, "Joe, Joe, DiMaggio, we want you on our side." Everybody was watching, hoping he would hit safely in one more game, waiting for him to miss. Every day for almost two months, Joe went out and got his hit. And not just one hit, either. He batted over .400 during the streak, which means that under pressure he was doing even better than he did ordinarily. After the streak finally ended—when third baseman Ken Keltner of the Indians made two great stops of smashes going past third—DiMaggio didn't stop. He went off on another sixteen-game hitting streak, which means that he hit safely in seventy-two out of seventy-three games. No ordinary ballplayer was ever under the pressure that Joe faced that season. No ordinary ballplayer could ever have reacted to it the way he did.

DiMaggio's exceptional courage in the face of pressure and discouragement really showed much later in his career, when he was getting old, as ballplayers go. He developed a bone spur in his heel, a very painful condition which makes it almost impossible to walk without pain. He played on it without complaint for a long time, but then it got so bad that it had to be operated on. In 1949 DiMaggio missed the first sixty-six games the Yankees played, almost half the season. He didn't get into the lineup until June, when the Yankees opened a series in Boston against the Red Sox, who were their biggest rivals at that time. When a man is out of action all season and everyone else has been playing since Opening Day, you expect him to take a few days to hit his stride. In that crucial series, DiMaggio hit his stride as soon as he went on the field.

The Yankees were held scoreless in their first time at bat, but DiMaggio led off the top of the second with a single. Another man walked and Hank Bauer hit a home run and the Yankees were ahead, 3–0, with DiMaggio scoring the first run. The next inning he came up again, with a man on base, and hit a home run. He made out the next time up, but in the eighth he walked and, spur or no spur, slid hard into second to break up a double play. And, after the Red Sox rallied to close the score to 5–4 in the ninth inning, with the tying run on base and Ted Williams up, he made a nice catch of Williams' long fly to end the game.

The next day the Red Sox jumped out to a 7–1 lead, but in the fifth inning DiMaggio came to bat with two men on. He got his pitch and hit a three-run homer over the left field wall to make the score 7–4. The Yankees were back in the game, and they went on to tie the score at 7–7. DiMaggio came up again in the eighth with two out and the bases empty. What did he do? He hit another home run, and the Yankees won again.

It was almost unbelievable. He hadn't been able to play all year but he came back as though he'd never been away. On the third day the Yankees took a 3–2 lead, but the Red Sox kept pressuring them. In the top of the eighth New York got two men on base and DiMaggio came to bat. The count went to three-and-two and then Joe split the game wide open with another three-run homer. The Yankees won 6–3 to sweep the series.

Even the fans in Boston cheered Joe. It was one of the greatest displays of clutch hitting that had ever been seen anywhere.

Joe's last year was 1951, which was my first with the Yankees. He had slowed up, and physically just wasn't the ballplayer he had been. He decided to retire after the World Series (it takes a little gumption to stick to that decision once you make it, especially when your salary is as big as Joe's was, but he stuck to it). The Yanks were playing the Giants.

DiMaggio had had a bad year (he hit only .263), and in the first three games in the Series he went to bat eleven straight times without a hit. The Yankees lost two of those three games. DiMag hated the idea of going out of baseball on a sour note. He was very proud in his quiet way. So, once again in the clutch, under pressure, knowing that this was his last time around, he came through. He had a home run and a single and drove in two runs in the fourth game of the Series. He had three hits, including a double, and three runs batted in in the fifth game. He had a double and two walks in four times at bat in the sixth game. He had six hits in twelve official times at bat in those last three games, with a home run, two doubles, and five runs batted in, and the Yankees swept the three games to win the Series.

When the chips were down, DiMaggio made himself come through.

Ted Williams was very different from Joe DiMaggio in most ways. His personality was explosive, where DiMaggio's was quiet. He was colorful; DiMaggio was not. DiMaggio was an all-around player; Ted's claim to greatness was entirely in his bat, though he was a far better fielder and baserunner than a lot of people ever realized.

But Williams was exactly like DiMaggio in one way. He proved his greatness when it was hard for him even to play, let alone play well. He came back from as many tough breaks as any player in the history of the game. Many players have had injuries or other things happen to them that slow them and interrupt their careers; a lot of them come back. But no one ever came back as often as Williams did and still do as well. After four seasons in the majors, he spent three years in service during World War II, as a Marine flier. After he came back to baseball he broke his elbow in 1950, and two years later he was called back to the Marines for the Korean conflict and missed most of two seasons. The year after that he broke his collarbone on the first day of spring training. Yet he ended his career third in lifetime home runs, behind Babe Ruth and Jimmy Foxx, and he was fifth among modern players in lifetime batting average. He had 521 home runs in his career; if he had been able to play ball those five seasons he spent with the Marines, and if he did about as well as he did during his other baseball years, he would have ended his career with close to seven hundred home runs and more than thirty-five hundred hits. And if that had happened, I think everybody would have recognized him as the greatest hitter in the history of baseball.

But even losing those years and having to come back, Ted maintained a consistently good record. He led the American League in batting six times: in 1941 and 1942, 1947 and 1948, and again in 1957 and 1958. He was the oldest player ever to win a batting championship. He batted .406 in 1941 when he was twenty-three and .388 in 1957 when he was thirty-nine. That is amazing consistency, particularly when you remember how many times his career was interrupted.

Ted had a lot of guts. When he hit .406 in 1941 he came into the last day of the season with 179 hits in 448 official at bats. That's an average of just under .400—or .39955, to be exact. In baseball, if your average is more than halfway between two figures—and Ted's was more than halfway between .399 and .400—you're given the higher figure. So Ted was listed at .400 and that's the way it would have gone into the record books. His manager suggested that he sit out the doubleheader scheduled for that last day of the season to make sure his average stayed at .400. It was a rare feat to hit .400 (it hadn't been done for eleven years before that and it hasn't been done since), and he was told not to take the chance of having a bad day and dropping down a few points.

But Williams said, "If I'm going to be the batting champion, I'm going to win it like a champion." He played both games of the doubleheader, and got six hits in eight times at bat to lift his average six points on the last day of the season, to the .406 figure. That took the courage of confidence.

In 1950 in the All-Star Game, Williams crashed into a wall as he made a fine running catch of a ball hit by Ralph Kiner of the National League, and broke his elbow. That happened in the first inning, but Williams did not leave the game until the ninth, and in the meantime he had singled and driven in an important run. Ted was sidelined most of the rest of the season and when he did play his batting average dropped sharply. His elbow bothered him the next season, too. His batting averages those two years, when he was bothered by the elbow, were the two lowest of his career, with one exception. Even so, and despite the pain, he hit .317 and .318.

Joe D. and Ted W.

Ted went back into the Marines early in 1952, but he left hitting an even .400; after he came back late in the 1953 season he hit .407 in thirty-seven games and had thirteen home runs. He was in good physical shape again and really looking forward to 1954, when he would have neither an injured elbow nor fighting a war on his mind. But in the first fifteen minutes of the first day of spring training he fell and broke his collarbone. He had to be operated on and a pin was inserted in his shoulder to hold things together when he got back to swinging a bat. That pin ached for a long time but Ted got back into the Red Sox lineup, and his averages over the next five years were magnificent. He hit .345, .356, .345, .388, and .328. He won the batting championship the last two years of that run. He didn't play quite enough games to be eligible for the batting championship in 1954 and 1955, but in both years his average was higher than the official batting champion's, and in 1956 he missed by only eight points.

Then in 1959 his average fell to .254, the worst he had ever had in the majors by more than sixty points. He was just about washed up, everyone decided. But Ted Williams, like Joe DiMaggio, had self-respect and pride and courage. He wanted to go out like a champion, so he played one more season. At the age of forty-two he lifted his batting average sixty-two points to .316, hit twenty-nine home runs, and won acclaim as Comeback Player of the Year.

Ted played his last game on September 28, 1960, in Boston. It had been announced that this would be his last game, and the stands were crowded. On his last time at bat, Williams, under pressure for the millionth time in his career, came through again. He hit a home run deep into the bullpen in far right-center field. The crowd roared its appreciation as Ted Williams crossed home plate with his last home run, his last hit, his last play as a major leaguer.

You Think It's Easy to Umpire?

(Chapter 19)

I would like to say a word for the umpires (I'm apt to get run out of our clubhouse for this). I used to get madder at umpires than I do nowadays, though I can still get pretty rednecked when I think I've gotten a bad call. But the more I see of umpires the more I have to admire them. One of the reasons is this: when a ballplayer makes a bad play, he gets booed and hooted and yelled at. An umpire gets booed or hooted not only when he makes a bad call but when the crowd *thinks* he has made a bad call. When a ballplayer makes a really fine play, he gets cheered; even an opposing ballplayer will be cheered for a great fielding play in most parks. But when an umpire makes a good play—when he is in the right spot at the right time and makes the right call on a difficult and confusing play, nobody notices. Nobody cheers. Nobody even cares.

It's like a bank account. When a player gets booed, his morale goes down; but when he gets cheered it goes back up. An umpire gets booed, but he never gets cheered; how does he keep his morale up?

Self-respect, I suppose. Umpires know that what they are doing is vitally important to the game, that the game depends on their fairness and accuracy and good judgment. When an umpire does a good job and knows that he has done a good job and knows that the players and his fellow umps know, he has to feel good.

But it's not easy. It takes courage to stand out there and take abuse. It takes courage to make the right call at a time when you know it will make you look wrong. It takes courage to keep cool and fair when hot-tempered players and managers are yelling and shouting at you and pointing out what they think you've been doing wrong in that game, or in that season, or in your entire career, and with nobody ever taking your side.

For instance, now and then you see a photograph in the paper that pretty well shows that an umpire missed a call. I remember there was one printed during the 1952 World Series between the Yankees and the Dodgers which showed umpire Al Passarella calling Johnny Sain out at first although Sain has his foot on the bag and the throw is still in the air a couple of feet from first baseman Gil Hodges' mitt. And there was a famous incident in the 1948 World Series when shortstop Lou Boudreau and pitcher Bob Feller of the Cleveland Indians pulled a perfect pick-off play at second base and seemingly caught Phil Masi of the Braves as he dove back into second. But umpire Bill Steward called Masi safe and the next day just about every paper in the country ran a picture of the play. Stewart never admitted he was wrong, and maybe he wasn't. You can't always tell from photographs. He said, with sarcasm, "I didn't have time to study the photograph. I had to call the play. And I called it the way I saw it."

An umpire has to have a lot of inner strength to stand strong when he has made a mistake. A player can shrug off an error and make it up with a base hit an inning or so later; but no one keeps track of an umpire's good plays. And it isn't only major league umpires who have to face that situation. I know a storekeeper in a small town who likes to umpire; he was a really good athlete when he was a boy and a young man, and he likes to stay close to the game. So he umpires sandlot ball and softball and Little League. One summer evening a few years ago he was umpiring a softball game between two teams in the town league, two teams that were bitter rivals. They were good teams; some of the players had been in professional ball for a time. They played all out, and this game was for blood. Jack was umpiring behind the plate.

The game was very tight and it went into the last of the ninth all tied up, 2–2. With two outs, the home team's best hitter came to bat. The count went to two strikes and one ball. The second strike had been a foul behind the crowd, and someone retrieved the ball and tossed it back to the umpire. As he got ready to follow the next pitch he thought to himself, "I better stick this ball in my pocket so it won't be in my way." But as he started to put it in his pocket—and just as the pitcher was in the middle of his windup—Jack dropped the ball. It rolled next to the plate and so he yelled, "Time!" and bent to pick up the ball. But the pitcher went through with his delivery and the batter swung. He hit the ball down the left field line, past the leftfielder. He raced around the bases with the crowd yelling and screaming; the leftfielder got the ball finally and threw it in, but the batter crossed home plate standing up with what looked like the game-winning run.

Jack, the umpire, yelled, "No play. The run doesn't

count. I called time out." He was mobbed by the team that thought it had won. Jack said to the batter, "You heard me call time out, didn't you?" The batter said, "Yes, but he pitched the ball. And I hit it, so it counts."

Jack said, "No, it doesn't. If you had struck out it wouldn't have counted, and if you hit a home run it doesn't count. I called time."

They yelled, "But it was your fault. You dropped that ball."

Jack said, "Right. It was my fault. But that doesn't change it. I had to call time, and I did. The run doesn't count."

The argument lasted for about fifteen minutes before they got settled down. When they did, the big batter struck out, and the argument flared up again for a minute or so. The game went fourteen innings and then ("Thank the Lord," Jack used to say) the team that hit the home run that didn't count finally scored and won the game anyway.

During the argument Jack noticed that the league commissioner, who had been watching the game, quietly got up and drove off. He said later that he had to go home because he and his wife were expecting guests. But a story in the local newspaper on the game quoted him as saying that the umpire had made a mistake in judgment and that the home run should have counted. Jack sat down and wrote him a letter. He said the only way to umpire is the right way, by the rules, and that the rules say that if an umpire calls time before a pitch is delivered the pitch does not count. He added that the only thing an umpire has going for him is the authority to enforce the rules; he can't change them in the middle of a game. And he pointed out that the argument might not have lasted so long if the head of the league had stayed at the game and backed up his umpire.

Well, the league commissioner had courage, too, and decency. He called the newspaper man who had written the earlier story and showed him Jack's letter and said that Jack was right. And he added that the league was lucky to have umpires like Jack, who had the courage to do the right thing.

Another example of an umpire's courage in the face of angry players was that displayed by Bill Grieve of the American League late in 1949. Bill stood firm while anger raged around him, and he didn't lose his own temper or his sense of responsibility.

It was a very important game between the Yankees and the Red Sox. It had been a terribly close pennant race—the Yankees finally won it by beating the Red Sox two straight in the last two games of the season—and this game, just a week before the season ended, looked at the time as though it could be the most important game of the year.

The score was tied in the eighth inning. The Red Sox had Johnny Pesky on third base. The batter hit a slow hopper to Tommy Henrich, who was playing first base for the Yankees. Tommy fielded the ball and threw it home to try to cut off the run. It was not a force play and the Yankee catcher, Ralph Houk, had to tag Pesky. Ralph was the third-string catcher on the club that year but he was in this important game because injuries—the Yanks had something like seventy different injuries that season—had thinned the team out some. Henrich's throw was good, low and right to the plate, and Ralph took it with his glove about a foot off the ground just as Pesky came sliding in. It was a very close play, but the photographs I've seen make it look as though Pesky was out. Grieve called him safe, and that started one of the biggest explosions Yankee Stadium has ever seen.

Houk jumped up screaming. Ralph keeps his temper under control pretty well, but when he lets it go once in a while it goes to the moon. He was absolutely convinced that Pesky was out, and he raged at Grieve. He danced around him like an Indian. He threw his glove down. He shouted. He yelled. He kept going around and around Grieve, bumping against him in his anger and excitement. Casey Stengel came off the bench and started yelling at Grieve, too, shouting and waving his arms, and he bumped the umpire, too. Other players and coaches gathered around. Joe Page, the Yankee pitcher, threw his glove high in the air in disgust. Now, if a player or a manager bumps an umpire he can be thrown out of the game on the spot. Same thing if a player throws a glove or a bat in the air because of an umpire's decision—you're gone.

Grieve had every right to throw Casey and Ralph and Joe Page out of the game. But he knew that this was a key game in the pennant race. He knew that Houk was the last catcher that Stengel had, and that Page was an important pitcher. He did not want to throw them out of a game as important as this one. And the same with Stengel, the manager. Grieve listened to them yell at him, tried to reason with them and calm them down, and finally did. Nobody was tossed out. Grieve had had the courage not to let his personal annoyance get in the way of a game as important as this one was. And don't think, as I once heard someone say, that he didn't throw anybody out because he knew he had made a mistake. I think it's when an umpire feels that he might have made a mistake that he is most apt to jump on a player. It's human nature, I guess. Ballplayers do the same thing.

Anyway, Grieve took all that yelling and pushing without losing his temper, and the game went on. The Red Sox won it, on Pesky's run. The Yankees were still steaming, and as the umpires went through the runway from the dugout to their dressing room, the Yankees got on Grieve all over again. Then one player, Cliff Mapes, shouted, "How much did you have on the game?"

That's when Grieve got angry. He could be patient when angry players in a tense game were blowing off steam. He could listen quietly to players saying that he had made a mistake, that he had booted one. But he could not allow a player to question his honesty and his integrity. He didn't laugh that one off. When the league office got his report on the incident Mapes was fined two hundred dollars and ordered to apologize to Grieve, which Cliff did, explaining that he really didn't mean what he said. Stengel and Houk were both fined, too, for bumping the umpire, but their fines were only one hundred dollars.

You have to admire a man like Bill Grieve, who had the courage not to get angry at one point where it would have been easy to blow his stack, and who had just as much courage at another point where it would have been easy to shrug Mapes' remark off. He knew his job and his duty in both instances.

Umpires are brave men. In the minor leagues, they have

been badly hurt by angry crowds and abandoned by guards and police who were supposed to give them protection after a game. They have had teeth knocked out, been hit by bottles, had their clothes ripped, have had air let out of their tires, have had sand poured in the crankcases of their cars, and in two instances, more than sixty years ago, have been killed. In the majors they travel constantly —they don't have long home stands the way players do— and during those long hot afternoons in July and cold night games in April they are out on the field the whole time, for both halves of every inning, with few chances to sit down in a dugout and rest for a spell. They work hard and they do a good job, and nobody notices.

Brave and Honest Hutch

(*Chapter 20*)

Courage is so much a part of some people's nature that you almost forget about it—until something happens that jars you into a new realization of it. Take Fred Hutchinson.

In 1937, when he was eighteen, Hutch was a great pitching star in the Pacific Coast League (he won twenty-five games and lost seven), which in itself was quite an achievement. The Pacific Coast League was a very fast league in the days before the majors expanded to California. It was about the closest thing to big league baseball that you could find. There were plenty of good young players on the way up, and plenty of good older players on the way down, who could have been playing still in the majors, except that they enjoyed being regulars in the Coast League more than they did sitting on the bench in the big leagues. For a kid of eighteen to star in this company took not only ability but toughness, heart, and competitive drive.

Fred Hutchinson had all of that, and some to spare. He was a determined man even then. His father was a doctor in Seattle and Hutch's brother Bill followed in his father's path and studied medicine, too. But Fred decided early that he wanted to be a ballplayer, and I guess that settled that. According to people from Seattle, when a Hutchinson makes up his mind there isn't much that anyone can do to change it.

There is a famous story about Fred's father that illustrates this. The doctor, who died several years ago, was a community leader, and back when Seattle still had trolley cars he was in the front of a running battle that went on about fare raises. It seems that the trolley company raised the fare and that Dr. Hutchinson and other people didn't care for the idea. There were protest meetings and petitions, and committees were sent to municipal hearings and all that sort of thing. Nothing much happened and the fight died down. Except for Dr. Hutchinson. He wasn't about to give in.

One night he was downtown and he got on a trolley car to go back home to the Hutchinsons' neighborhood, which was several miles away. He dropped the old fare (I think it was a nickel) in the box. The driver said, "Sorry. The fare has been raised." It was now a dime, let's say. Dr. Hutchinson said, "This is the fare I have always paid." The driver shrugged his shoulders and said, "I'm sorry, but it's been raised." Dr. Hutchinson said, "You mean, the money I have put in there is not enough?" The driver said, "That's right." Dr. Hutchinson said, "You mean, if I don't pay more I will have to get off and walk home?" The driver said, "I guess so." Dr. Hutchinson said, "Give me back my money." The driver did and Dr. Hutchinson got off the trolley and walked home.

But he didn't just walk home. He walked home on the trolley tracks, right in front of the trolley. It was his way of calling attention to the dispute over the fares, and he made the most of it. The trolley couldn't get past him, and it wasn't going to knock him down and run over him, and nobody was going to move Dr. Hutchinson off the tracks. (Knowing Fred, I can believe that; anyone who ever saw Hutch get mad will tell you that a Hutchinson is not a man to mess with.)

The doctor walked home, his head high and his jaw out, and all the trolleys on the line piled up behind him, trailing along like a kid's wooden choo-choo train, and they didn't get moving on normal schedule again until Dr. Hutchinson reached home and walked off the street. I don't know what the result was—I guess the fare stayed raised—but I know this, that of all the people involved in the fuss over the trolley fare, Dr. Hutchinson fought longest and hardest and best. He was a man who believed in his principles and he didn't give in.

His son Fred had the same qualities from the time he first played baseball. He was brought up to the major leagues by the Detroit Tigers before he was twenty, and while he never was as great a star in the majors as he was in the minors, he was a key man on the Tiger staff for several years. He was also a good hitter, which figures, because most of all Hutch was a competitor, a man who was never afraid of the idea of winning and who would do everything he could to win. Some people are kind of afraid of winning; the idea of trying hard to win seems to embarrass them. Not Hutch. Winning was what he expected to do. Losing was a mistake.

When Fred was named manager of the Detroit Tigers in 1952, people who didn't know him were surprised. For one thing, he was young—only thirty-three. For a second, he had had no managing or coaching experience. And for a third, he was a pitcher—and very few major league managers have been pitchers. Lots of catchers and infielders have been managers, and some outfielders, but only a handful of pitchers.

But to everybody who knew Hutch, it seemed absolutely right. As a manager he was a natural, a man others looked up to. There have been few men in baseball who have been praised as a man by as many people as Hutchinson. It isn't just that everybody liked him—a lot of baseball players are well liked by their teammates and by managers and by the front office and by fans, and yet do not have the qualifications of a manager. A manager has to be respected, too, and no one was ever more respected than Hutch.

He got the Tigers from last place to fifth in a couple of seasons. Later, he managed the St. Louis Cardinals and moved them from seventh to second in two years. He took over the Cincinnati Reds when they were in the second division—two seasons later they won the National League pennant.

All this doesn't mean that Hutch was the greatest manager ever to run a major league team, but nobody ever got more out of his players. It's probably because Hutch was always completely honest with everybody—and players know that. Hutch was never afraid to speak his mind —to anybody—and he didn't sneak around corners to do it. It takes a lot of courage to be honest all the time. Think of the times when you've bent the truth a little to get out of an awkward or embarrassing situation.

There was a time when Hutch was managing the Cardinals when he had a run-in with August A. Busch, Jr., the owner of the team. Mr. Busch was concerned with the Cardinals' attendance, which had fallen off a bit, and he was bothered because the Cardinals were not as colorful a team as they used to be. He wanted a good team, but he wanted a colorful team, too. Now, the Cardinals had a rookie first baseman at that time, a very tall, graceful guy who had a strange way of fielding his position. He would stretch his arms out wide, like a net, and if there was a chance of a bunt, say, he would sort of crouch and lean over and as the pitcher threw he would come scurrying in toward the plate.

It was a wild sight, this big tall man bent over with his arms spread, racing in across the infield. The crowd loved it. The only thing was, the first baseman wasn't much of a ballplayer. He had had several chances and had proved that he couldn't hit major league pitching, and Hutch benched him.

A few days later Mr. Busch and Frank Lane, who was general manager of the Cardinals then, and Hutch, and perhaps a couple of other club officials, had a meeting to discuss the team. Mr. Busch kept bringing up the name of the rookie first baseman. Hutch said he wasn't good enough. Busch thought maybe they should play him anyway because the crowd enjoyed seeing him in the field, the way he spread his arms and all. Hutch said he couldn't hit, that he wasn't a major league ballplayer. Busch said maybe so, but he certainly was colorful and the crowd got a lot of laughs out of him and perhaps the Cardinals should play him anyway. Hutch looked at Mr. Busch, who was his boss, you remember, and said, "If you want a clown to play first base, why don't you hire Emmett Kelly?" (Kelly was the famous sad-faced "bum" of the Ringling Brothers Barnum and Bailey circus.) That sort of ended the meeting. It wasn't a polite answer, and it certainly wasn't diplomatic. But it was honest. And Hutch was right. The colorful first baseman never did make it in the majors.

When you are as honest as Hutch, you expect everybody else to be honest, too. And that means you *expect* a ballplayer to do his honest best, all the time. It takes effort, and it takes courage, to do your honest best all the time. I think every major league ballplayer *thinks* he is doing his best, but sometimes without realizing it a player will ease off and let down a little. But not if he was playing for a guy like Hutchinson. Not for long.

A fellow named Jim Davis, a good left-handed knuckleballer who pitched for the Cubs and the Cardinals and the Giants several years ago, once told a story about himself that showed how players felt about Hutchinson. Jim said, "I think I know why players do well for Hutch. I remember one game I was pitching, and we were a couple of runs ahead in the middle of the game. There was one out, and a fellow got a hit, and then I got behind on the next man. I was thinking to myself, if this guy gets on base I'll really have to bear down on that next batter. Then I happened to glance over at the dugout and there was Hutch, up on the top step, glaring at me. I thought to myself, oh boy, I better bear down on *this* guy or Hutch is gonna be out here. He made you work hard without saying anything."

Everybody in baseball knew Hutch from the time he

first broke in and knew the kind of man he always was. I guess we all took him for granted and forgot what a special man he was until something happened to remind us all over again. I mean his illness.

In early 1964 there was a story in the papers one day that said that Fred Hutchinson had had a physical examination and that something was wrong with his chest. Right away people who knew him began to worry, as you always do when you think something might be seriously wrong with someone you know well. Hutch flew from his home in Florida to Seattle to consult with his brother Bill, the doctor. He had chest X-rays and more examinations. Then a medical report was issued, stating that Hutch had a "malignancy" and that he would undergo special treatment.

I felt sick when I heard that. "Malignancy" means cancer. Some people wondered why the medical report was so outspoken, and they wondered if Hutch knew what he had.

They didn't have to wait long. Reporters were politely trying to find out more information. Instead of hiding, or staying out of sight someplace and letting his brother or some other doctor talk to the press, Fred Hutchinson talked to the reporters himself. He told them what the doctors had told him, what treatment he would undergo, what his chances were. He said he had found out about it at Christmastime and that it was like having a rug pulled out from under you. "One day you're fine," he said, "and the next day you have cancer." He didn't use the word "malignancy." He was still the same old Hutch. He grinned that little half grin of his at the reporters, told them the truth, and didn't try to fool them or himself or anybody.

It takes courage to be that honest. It takes courage, and lots of it, to be a man like Fred Hutchinson. Happily, courage like that rubs off on other people. One of the reporters said, "I thought I would feel sorry for Hutch. Instead, I feel—I don't know—proud. I feel proud to be a human being because Hutchinson is one. I mean, *he* has cancer but instead of letting me feel sorry for him he makes me feel good just because I know him. What a man he is."

Casey Never Quit

(*Chapter 21*)

I've got to tell you about Casey Stengel. Old Case was manager of the New York Yankees when they signed me up in 1949 when I wasn't even eighteen. He was manager when I went to the Yankees' instructional camp for young players in Phoenix in 1951. He was my first major league manager and my only one for the first ten years that I was in the majors. I got to know him pretty well. He used to get mad at me sometimes, and I guess I used to get a little mad at him once in a while, though I wouldn't show it when he was around.

He was a good manager—anybody who wins ten pennants in twelve years has to be good—and one of the smartest baseball men ever. He was also about the funniest person I've ever known, especially when he got off on one of those rambling speeches with all those winks and facial expressions.

I guess just about everybody knows that about Casey— I mean, that he's a smart baseball man, a successful manager, a funny person, and colorful and fun to watch, and all that. But there is something else impressive about him that not many people notice, unless they're around him a lot. And that's his courage. He's a brave man. He never quits.

It takes a good deal of real quality to keep from getting down in the mouth when you're beaten at something. I mean really beaten, in an important game or at an important time. I've noticed that often in baseball. Early in the season a team may get hot and challenge for the league lead. Then they go against another hot club and they lose a key game. All right, that's a hard game to lose. It's tough. But, as they say around baseball, when the going gets tough the tough get going. A club with heart comes back after defeat. But you'll notice that many teams after they've lost a tough game or a tough series keep on losing and fall right out of contention.

Now this doesn't mean that a good team that goes into a slump after a rough defeat is a gutless team. But it does mean that they let down. They may do it subconsciously, but they do it. And then another hot team comes along, or a relaxed team that's just aching to knock somebody off, and wham! The team that is down loses another. Now they get a little tight about it—and they lose another. Now they get a little nervous. They tense up. They try too hard. They lose again. And, blooey, they're in a real slump.

Coming back to win after a bitter defeat is one of the hardest things to do in sport. That goes for individuals, as well as teams. In baseball, if a batter gets the horsecollar against a certain pitcher, the next time he faces that pitcher he might find himself thinking about that. He gets a little too careful, wondering what the pitcher knows about his hitting weaknesses. Maybe he starts to outthink himself. If he goes down the drain again, he's in trouble against that pitcher. Before long, the pitcher dominates him. It's an old story: defeat breeds defeat.

Now to get back to Casey. He's an old man now, past seventy, and he's been in baseball for more than half a century. Most people think of him as one of the most successful managers in baseball history (despite the fact that he gained recent fame as the manager of the losing Mets). Some people remember that he used to manage second-division ball clubs (even before the Mets), and a few recall that he was a World Series star with the old New York Giants more than forty years ago.

But you go through the record books and talk to a few old-timers and you find out that Casey's long career has had a lot of ups and downs. You learn, too, that the downs never got *him* down. It's really amazing.

Casey broke into baseball in 1910 with Kankakee in the Northern Association. The league folded up in July and Casey was not only out of a job, he was out of a team and a league. He switched over to Maysville in the Blue Grass League (they had some strange-sounding leagues in those days), and in sixty-nine games he hit a measly .223. That's a pretty bad average in the majors. In the low minors it means you don't have much future.

What did Casey do? Pack up and go home and go back to that dental college everybody talks about? Nope. He came back the next year with Aurora in the Wisconsin-Illinois League and batted .352 to lead the league in hitting. He moved up to the Southern Association the next season, hit .290, and before the year was out he was in the big leagues with the Brooklyn Dodgers. Two years after he had hit .223 with Maysville, he was in the majors. That defeat (and I think you can call .223 a defeat) didn't get him down.

He had six seasons with the Dodgers, some of them pretty good ones, and played in one World Series, in 1916. That year Casey batted only .279 in regular-season play. In the Series he hit .364.

The year after the Dodgers won the pennant they fell to seventh place and Casey was traded to the Pittsburgh Pirates, who were in eighth place, and two years after that he was traded to the Philadelphia Phillies, who were also in last place. When a player keeps being traded by losing clubs he can sort of figure that he's near the end of the road. Some players give up and quit baseball when that happens. Casey didn't.

He batted .292 for the Phillies and caught the attention of John McGraw, manager of the New York Giants, who traded for him in the middle of the 1921 season. The Giants won the pennant and Casey batted .284, though he played only forty-two games all season. It was like a last little gasp for a good player. Except that Casey wasn't making his last gasp.

He became a valued part-time player for the Giants, and in the next two seasons batted .368 and .339 for them. Yet even with those averages, he did even better in the World Series in each of those years. He batted .400 in the World Series of 1922 and .417 in the Series of 1923. In the 1922 Series he had played in only two games (the Giants beat the Yanks four games to none, with one tie). But in 1923 he came roaring back again, played in all six Series games, and was the Giants' star. The Giants won only two games in that Series, and Casey won both of them with home runs. That was the first World Series ever played in Yankee Stadium, and Casey's were the first two

Series homers ever hit there. When I think of Ruth and Gehrig and DiMaggio and Berra and Maris and myself and all the other distance hitters who played in the Stadium in all the years since, it gives me a kick to realize that the old man was the first one ever to hit a home run there in the World Series. And then to realize that he went back two days later and hit the *second* home run ever hit there —well, I don't know. Old Casey—it's just what he would do.

After that, Casey's playing career finally began to peter out. He had one more full year in the majors and then went down to the minors to manage. He finished third, fourth, and first in his first three years of managing, but then defeat came raining down again. He finished sixth, eighth, and eighth in three of the next four years. Then he caught on as a coach with the Brooklyn Dodgers, and two years later became their manager. Brooklyn didn't have much of a team then and Casey finished sixth, fifth, and seventh. Then he got fired, and it was a humiliating way to get fired. The Dodger owners wanted to get rid of him so badly that they bought up the last year of his contract; that is, they paid him his full salary for a year *not* to manage.

After that he managed the old Boston Braves for six seasons. He finished fifth once, sixth once, and seventh four times, and was hooted and booed and criticized all the way. One year he was hit by a taxicab and broke his leg, and a Boston sports columnist wrote that the cab driver should get a reward for having done the most for Boston baseball. That was nice.

Casey went back down to the minors after that season. He was fifty-three years old. He had managed in the majors for nine seasons and had never even had a first-division team. He was down in the minors, managing, for five years.

Then, in a move that surprised everybody, the Yankees hired him as manager for the 1949 season. There was a lot of criticism. Casey was a clown, people said. He didn't know baseball. He had a terrible managerial record—look how poorly he did with the Dodgers and the Braves.

But people forgot that after Casey hit .223 with Maysville one year he led his league in batting the next. They forgot that after he was traded from a seventh-place club to an eighth-place club to an eighth-place club, he was traded to a pennant-winner and played and starred in two World Series. They forgot that after looking all washed up, he batted .368 and .339 in successive seasons. They forgot that Casey knew how to come back.

Stengel won his first pennant with the Yankees on the last day of the season. The next year he eked out a win over the Detroit Tigers. He won a third pennant with the Yankees in 1951, and a fourth in 1952, and a fifth in 1953. He won five straight World Series, the first time any team or any manager ever won five Series in a row.

His string was broken by the Cleveland Indians in 1954, but Casey and the Yankees came back and won four more pennants in a row, and after the White Sox won in 1959, he came back again for one last pennant before the Yankees retired him. And you know how, after a year on the sidelines, he came back to action again with the Mets (and knowing Casey, I wouldn't bet too much against the Mets; you never can tell).

All through his career, Casey had this comeback courage. Defeat *never* got him down. He hated to lose, but he never let it get to him. All it did was make him fight harder.

I particularly remember the 1958 World Series. We were playing the Milwaukee Braves, and they had beaten us the year before. They had practically the same team back again, a powerful club with Spahn and Burdette and Aaron and Mathews and all those fellows. They beat us 4–3 in the tenth inning of the first game and then racked us up 13–5 in the second game. We came back to New York for the third game and beat them 4–0, but in the fourth game of the Series everything fell apart.

Warren Spahn pitched a two-hit shutout against us, and though Whitey Ford was pitching almost as good a game for us, we kicked it away in the field. It was awful. Our left fielder lost a high fly ball in the sun and it fell safely for a triple. Our infield moved in to cut off the run at the plate, and our shortstop bobbled the ground ball that was hit at him and the run scored. A couple of innings later there was another high fly to left and—unbelievably—our left fielder lost this one in the sun, too, and another run scored.

I think that was the lowest point the Yankees ever reached in my career with them. I mean, we've been beaten now and then, but never—not even in the 1963 World Series when the Dodgers took us in four straight games—did we look so bad, so butterfingered, so plain terrible. We looked as though our morale was shot, and I imagine a lot of the fans felt that the Series was as good as gone.

Not Casey. Even though the Braves now had a three-to-one lead in the Series, and had to win only one of the three games left to become World Champions for the second straight year. Right then, right when the roof was falling in and fly balls were dropping and runs were scoring, that's when old Stengel ran up the dugout steps and started shouting at us. He wasn't bawling us out. He was rolling his arms in front of his chest in that old gesture of his that meant, "Let's go get them!" We were getting the sawdust beaten out of us, but there he was on top of the steps yelling and shouting at us as though we were putting on a rally. He was saying, Don't quit. We'll get 'em.

We should have been through after that game, but Stengel wouldn't let us be through. He was rallying us around and planning his pitching for two and three games ahead. The next day we faced Lew Burdette, who had beaten us in four successive World Series games over two years. We knocked him out of the box and beat Milwaukee 7–0.

Stengel took us back to Milwaukee and there we beat Warren Spahn 4–3 in ten innings in one of the most exciting games I can remember. Now it was all tied up, and Casey had us rolling. Nothing was going to stop us now. I suppose the seventh game looked close on the surface until Moose Skowron hit a three-run homer in the eighth, but I don't believe anybody on the Yankees had any doubts at all. Casey had brought us back from defeat, and we knew we were going to win.

Casey didn't hit for us, and Casey didn't pitch for us, and, for sure, he didn't field for us. But that comeback drive of his, that don't-quit spirit, had a lot to do with the Yankee victory that year.

As one sportswriter said after that Series, "Defeat does not awe Casey, and he is on good terms with hope." That's another way of saying that he wasn't scared of what happened, and he wasn't scared of what might happen. That's another way of saying that Casey Stengel is a man of courage.

The Iron Major

(*Chapter 22*)

I have played with and against some of the best players in the history of baseball—men like Joe DiMaggio, Ted Williams, Stan Musial, Willie Mays, Yogi Berra, Whitey Ford, Jackie Robinson, Bob Feller, Sandy Koufax, Duke Snider . . . I don't have space to begin to name them all. I have played under or against some of the finest managers the game ever saw—Casey Stengel, Al Lopez, Leo Durocher, Walter Alston, Fred Hutchinson, Paul Richards . . . again, the list is long.

I admire all these men. You always have a special regard for the best in your own field. My business is baseball, and these men are the best in my business, and I admire them very much.

But the man I guess I admire more than anybody else in baseball played in only ninety-one big league games, not much more than half a season. And he managed for only three years. Connie Mack managed for more than fifty years. Casey Stengel has managed, off and on, for more than thirty.

His name is Ralph Houk. If you think it's odd for a man like me, with more than a dozen years in the majors, more than four hundred home runs, one batting championship, three Most Valuable Player awards, and all the blown-up publicity that a big-name player always gets . . . if you think it's odd for me to have such a high regard for Ralph Houk, then you just don't know the man. I'd like to tell you about him.

First of all, Ralph entered World War II as a private and came out as a major. He deserved that high rank, because Ralph is a leader of men. He had to be to command a Ranger battalion in the war. And I know that he was when he managed the Yankees to three straight pennants in the three years he managed us. It's the only perfect record—a championship every year he managed—I ever heard of for managing in the majors.

The only war stories Ralph usually tells are the funny ones, the comical things that sometimes happen even in the middle of a bloody, ugly war. But the laughs were only a small part. Ralph had nightmares the first six months he was back from the war, as a lot of other combat soldiers did, and if what happened was bad enough to give a man with the courage Houk has bad dreams, it had to be grim.

Once, against his better judgment, Ralph had to take a force of Rangers across a river and into a town that was under German attack. He studied the maps and pointed out to his commander why he thought it was a bad move. But the orders were not changed, and Houk had to go into the town. He had only one way in, over a bridge. The Germans had three roads on the other side over which they could enter. Ralph took thirty-four men, an armored car, a light tank, and other bits of equipment and went over the bridge into the town. As soon as the Americans were in, the German artillery blew up the bridge behind them and started battering the town. The Americans were trapped.

Reinforcements couldn't get to them because the bridge was gone, and the enemy was able to move into the town from different angles. The entire group should have been wiped out—either killed or captured. But Houk got more than a third of his men out safely, swimming back across the river.

Another time, when American troops under General McAuliffe were trapped at Bastogne during the Battle of the Bulge, Houk had to take a patrol through the German lines to Bastogne to get information on the number of men there, their equipment, condition, and so on. Then he had to go back through the German lines to American headquarters with that information. He had orders to destroy the papers he was carrying if there was a chance that he'd be captured or killed. Houk made it safely both ways. He won the Silver Star.

There were a lot of things. One time he was hit by a bullet that went into the back part of his helmet and out the front. He never knew how it missed his head, but he kept the helmet as a souvenir. It had a clean hole in the back and a ragged hole in the front.

Ralph must have been quite a soldier, quite an officer. Knowing him as I do, I can believe that his men would do anything for him.

Houk showed courage later when he went back to baseball. He had a good minor league record, but he never got a chance to play much for the Yankees, who had fine catchers like Aaron Robinson and then Yogi Berra ahead of him. Ralph was on the Yankee roster for eight seasons, but got into only ninety-one games. He didn't object because he knew he was contributing to the club as a part-time player and as a bullpen catcher; and in preparation for his later career as a manager, he was learning more and more about major league baseball. He was getting himself ready for the break that had to come his way some day. And that is something to remember. A lucky break doesn't mean anything unless you are ready to take advantage of it. Branch Rickey said once, "Luck is the residue of design." What that means is, if you get everything ready luck has to come your way. And what *that* means is, everybody gets lucky breaks some time or other, but a lot of people never notice them because they're not ready for them.

Houk was ready when his time came—when Casey Stengel was retired as Yankee manager after the 1960 season. He knew he could manage, and he knew he would manage some day, so he got himself ready ahead of time.

But Ralph always had confidence in himself, and the courage that goes with that confidence. In one of his first years with the Yankees, when he was told that he was being sent back down to the minors again—even though he had had a good season in the farm system the previous year—he got stubborn. He was convinced that he deserved to be in the majors. He refused to report to the Yankee farm club he had been assigned to, and he stayed at the Yankee spring training camp for four days to argue his point. Finally, he said, "I'm good enough to play in the majors. If you don't think so, give me my release. If not, I'm going to retire from baseball."

Now, a lot of ballplayers occasionally threaten to quit, but they're usually not too serious. Houk was. He was about thirty and he felt that there was no future for him in being a minor league ballplayer at that age. He felt that if he wasn't going to make it as a major leaguer, he would have to go back home to Kansas and get a job with a future. He was so serious and his argument was so strong that George Weiss, then general manager of the Yankees, sat down and talked to him. Weiss could be a pretty tough man with a ballplayer who was just shooting off his mouth, but he knew Houk was a serious man and a smart one, too. He explained the situation to Houk, that the Yankees had no room for him that year but that there was a definite place for him in the Yankee organization in the future, if not as a player, then as a coach and manager.

Ralph had the courage, too, not to be afraid to change his position. What he was arguing for, what he was asking for, was recognition of his abilities. Weiss recognized them and told Houk he recognized them. Ralph agreed to go to the minors. He came back up to the Yankees, had to go down once again, but then came up to stay for several pennant-winning seasons, studying and learning baseball all that time.

When his playing career was about over, the Yankees made Ralph manager of their top minor-league farm club. He took over the job and did so well in the three seasons he was there that he was brought back up to the Yankees as a coach under Casey Stengel. And when Casey left, it was obvious that Ralph was the man to take his place. He had had an offer to manage Detroit, but he checked that offer with the Yankees and then waited. That took patience, turning down one job to wait for another. Patience takes courage, too.

And then, when he got the Yankee job, it wasn't easy

stepping into Casey's shoes. Stengel had won ten pennants in twelve years and was recognized as a baseball genius. Houk was under great pressure. When Yogi Berra succeeded Ralph in 1964, Yogi was a famous baseball name in his own right as a player. But when Ralph succeeded Casey, he was a nobody taking over for the best-known man in baseball. He had to win or be dismissed as a minor leaguer in a major leaguer's shoes.

He won, but it wasn't as easy as that. We started off badly for him—as we did for Yogi at the beginning of 1964 —and there were a lot of problems for him to solve. Along with things like batting orders and the pitching rotation, he had to prove that he was the manager of the ball club. Ralph did things quietly and he used less direct discipline than Casey did, but he made it clear that he was the boss, and nobody questioned that for a minute. More than that, he made his players respect themselves in respecting him.

I'll try to tell you what I mean. I played for Casey for ten seasons, and he was very good to me. He took me in hand when I was nineteen and he taught me a great deal about the game. Under him I became a major league player.

But I think I was always sort of a disappointment to Casey. He wanted me to be the greatest player in the world, and I wasn't. One of Casey's ways to get a man to play better was to criticize him. It's hard to say that that system doesn't work—after all, Casey has those ten pennants as proof—but sometimes it made me feel pretty low. When Ralph took over as manager, he didn't say anything at all about hoping that I would finally develop into the outstanding player I should be. Instead, he said that I *was* an outstanding player right now, that I was a player the other players on the team respected and looked to as a leader.

That might not seem like very much, but to me it meant a great deal. Houk said that I was the team leader, the man that the other players looked to. I took that seriously. It meant that Ralph was relying on me, and I felt the responsibility. I stopped moaning and feeling sorry for myself. I'm not proud of it but I used to sulk, especially if we lost a close game or I had a bad day. The newspapermen could tell you that I was pretty hard to get along with sometimes. But if I was the team leader, I had to act like one. The Yankees have a secret weapon, you know, and that secret weapon is teamwork, respect for one another's ability. Even more than in the past, I felt that the team was more important than I was. I felt the responsibility. And I feel that Ralph Houk made a man out of me.

The thing about all this is that Ralph had the courage to change things, to run the ball club his way. He learned a lot playing and coaching under Casey, and he used a lot of what he learned in running the Yankees himself. But he didn't try to ape Casey in strategy and tactics. He wasn't afraid to do things his own way.

Of course, you'd expect that a man who had won the Silver Star in a war would not be afraid to assert himself. But Houk had had the courage and common sense a long time before to look ahead and figure out what he would have to do to be ready for whatever came. When it did come, he was ready. That was a break for me and a break for the Yankees, too. How many clubs could follow a manager like Stengel with a manager like Houk? When the club moved Ralph up to the front office in the fall of 1963 as general manager, the top job in the organization after the owners, it was a tribute to one of the finest men I've ever known, and one of the bravest.

Last Inning

(Chapter 23)

I have been pretty lucky all my life, in most ways. I came from a poor section of the country and was born in the Depression and my family had to struggle to come through okay, and yet I have made a lot of money in my life, enough to take care of not only my wife and my four sons, but my mother and my sister and my brothers when they were younger. I have made enough so that worries over money should never bother me or my family. Money isn't everything, but as a poor boy once I can tell you that you can't get away from the fact that not having money can cause an awful lot of misery. So I've been lucky that way.

I was lucky, too, in an athletic way, in that I grew big early. Sport is an important part of any boy's life, and being too small to play a game well is enough to make some boys very unhappy. I never had that. I always knew that I would be good enough to play. When I was fifteen, for instance, I played baseball with grown men. I signed a professional contract with the New York Yankees when I was only seventeen. I was in the majors when I was nineteen and played in a World Series before I was twenty. So I was lucky that way—in that I didn't have a long, hard struggle to get to the major leagues.

I think of Harry Bright, who joined the Yankees in 1963 and did so much to help us win the pennant. Harry and I played in the same minor league in 1949, when I was seventeen and he was nineteen. Harry had already played a season or so of minor league ball and was a star of the league. I did well—I had seven homers, sixty-three runs batted in, and a .313 batting average, but Harry led the league in runs batted in and had ten homers and a .286 average. I was a shortstop, and Harry played third base and second base. Two years later I was in the majors. Harry didn't get there for nine years—or until just before his twenty-ninth birthday. In the meantime he had moved on to minor league teams in Sioux Falls, South Dakota; Clovis, New Mexico; Topeka, Kansas; Janesville, Wisconsin; Memphis, Tennessee; Buffalo, New York; Little Rock, Arkansas and Sacramento, California. Harry had a long, hard trip to the majors, even though he was a good player all the way, as he finally proved when he made it. I had it easy. I was lucky.

I was lucky, too, that I joined the Yankees. I was in a World Series my first year and in eleven in my first thirteen seasons. A lot of fine players never have gotten in a World Series—Al Kaline is an example—and others have never been in more than one or two, like Ted Williams and Hank Aaron.

I have had good managers—Casey Stengel and Ralph Houk and Yogi Berra. I had good managers in the minors, too. My first manager was Harry Craft, who went on up to manage Kansas City in the American League and then Houston in the National. He was wonderful to me. He did so much to help me along when I was just a green kid.

I could have had somebody who was too busy to worry about young players, or who simply didn't care. I was lucky. I had Harry Craft.

I was lucky to have such a good family behind me. My father and mother always had to scrape and scramble to bring us up, but they did it, and without complaining. They did it so that we never realized that we were missing anything. And I don't guess we did miss anything that was too important. We didn't have TV and transistors and sports cars and new clothes. But we had food to eat, we liked each other, and we had fun.

So I have been pretty lucky all my life, and I will never forget that I have been. But nothing is all luck, or all good. You know how they say that the grass always looks greener in the other fellow's yard. That's true. No matter how good things go for you, you sometimes envy somebody else. At the same time, no matter how good something is going for somebody else, there's always something that isn't so good. With all my luck and good fortune and success, I have had some really bad things happen, things that hurt, that made me feel at times like the unluckiest man in the world.

Worst of all was my father dying just as I got to the major leagues. I loved my dad and I would have loved to have had him around to see me play ball all these years. Every man who likes baseball dreams a little that his son will be a baseball star. My dad didn't just like baseball— he was crazy about it. He talked to me and coached me and worked with me from the time I was a little kid, all with the hope that I'd become a big-leaguer. And then when I made it, he couldn't be there—except for that first season—to watch and enjoy it.

Then there was another bad thing. When my father died I was twenty years old. I had just gotten married. My twin brothers were only about fifteen, and my sister and my little brother were younger than that. I had had only one season in the majors, and during that season I had to go back down to the minors for a while. With the Yankees I had batted only .267, and in the World Series had fallen and hurt my knee so badly that I had to go to the hospital for an operation. I wasn't an established major-league ballplayer. I still had a long way to go to prove myself—but here I was, a twenty-year-old kid with six people depending on him—my wife, my mother, my three younger brothers, and my sister. I don't mind telling you the thought of that scared me more than a little. If I didn't come through in baseball, I would really let them down. I don't mean I'd disappoint them just because I didn't make it as a baseball player. I mean there wouldn't be any money to pay for food and clothes and rent.

And then there were the injuries. It seems funny to say it, but despite the fact that I grew big early and that I have speed and strength and all the things you want from a good physique, I have been troubled with injuries and ailments all my adult life. I suppose that having a bad knee or an abscess or something like that would be a nuisance to any grown man trying to earn a living. When you are a professional athlete earning your living with the strength and skills of your body, pains and aches are more than a nuisance. They're a threat. And I have been threatened, it seems, practically every year that I have been in the majors. Some doctors think it's surprising that I have lasted as a player as long as I have. Like Al Kaline, I had osteomyelitis, a disease of the bone marrow, before I came into baseball. I don't know for sure if that's the reason I have had so much trouble with my legs during my career, but I guess it must have something to do with it. All I know is that some days my legs ache so much that I hate the thought of playing. But you have to. You have to make yourself do what you have to do.

The first really bad thing to happen to me physically was hurting my knee in the 1951 World Series at the end of my first season in the majors. After being sent down to the minors in July that year, I came back up in the middle of August to stay, but was still only a part-time player, part of Casey Stengel's platoon system. I was surprised when he started me in the first game of the Series, surprised and pleased. I felt as though I had really arrived at last.

Then in the fifth inning of the second game, it happened. Willie Mays was up (he was in his rookie year, too), and hit a hard fly to right center. I was playing right field and ran hard to my right to get the ball. Joe Di-Maggio was playing center—it was his last year—and he cut to his left, deeper and behind me, to back me up. I was going all out for the ball, giving it everything I had, when suddenly my right knee snapped. I tumbled and fell. DiMaggio made a great play—talk about grace under pressure—by shifting his course at the last instant and moving in behind me to catch the ball as I fell. They came out with a stretcher and carried me off the field and eventually to the hospital. It took five long months for my knee to heal, and it never has been really right since. If I put a certain kind of twisting pressure on it, it will pop right out. That's why I have to tape my legs every day before a game, to hold the knee and other things in place.

I've pulled muscles in my thighs at different times so badly that I've been put out of action. A lot of athletes suffer from pulled muscles—runners especially, I guess— but I don't know, when I do it, it always turns out to be serious. A doctor said once that it was because I have exceptional strength in certain driving muscles—in the legs and arms and back—and when I explode all that strength into something—like throwing a ball or swinging a bat or running full speed—I put too much of a strain on other parts of my body, like ligaments and cartilages and smaller muscles, and I tear things. Of course, you can't think about that when you're trying to beat out a base hit or catch a runner trying to score, but it's always sort of hanging around in the back of my mind. It's a constant worry.

I missed most of the 1955 World Series between the Yankees and the Dodgers because of a bad leg. I missed one game and most of another in the 1957 Series against the Milwaukee Braves after I hurt my shoulder when Red Schoendienst and I banged together at second base. I missed part of the 1961 Series against the Cincinnati Reds because of an abscess on my hip. That was bad luck all the way. I had a bad cold that I couldn't shake and to try to get rid of it I went to a doctor and got a shot of an anti- biotic. But something happened—I don't know for sure just what—and an abscess formed deep inside my hip, almost to the bone. It had to be drained and it wouldn't heal, and every time I did something strenuous, like run- ning hard after a fly ball or taking a big cut at a pitch, it would rip open again and start to bleed. That was the year, you remember, when Roger Maris hit sixty-one home runs and I hit fifty-four. I had to sit out the last few games of the season. I wouldn't have caught up to Roger even if I had been okay, but I would have been able to play the whole Series against the Reds—not that the Yanks needed me that year.

The next year, 1962, was miserable and great, all at the same time. We won the pennant and we beat the Giants in the World Series and I won the Most Valuable Player award. But I had a lot of trouble physically, particularly with my legs. One day I was trying to beat out an infield grounder and really raced down the line toward first base. Just as I got to the base something popped in my thigh. My head went up in the air and I went down like a log. I looked as though I'd been shot. It was a muscle pull, one of the worst I ever had. I was out of action for a long time.

But I got over it and played in the World Series, and the next spring in training in Florida it felt fine. I had a good spring and when the season opened I felt great. I was hoping that I could stay in one piece for the whole year and really put together a good season. One reason, of course, was for myself, but another was for Ralph Houk. I wanted to be able to give Ralph my best for a full season, every day if possible. I felt real good the first couple of days. Then it started. One day when I was playing center field a man hit a fly ball to left center. I ran over and caught it and just as I did somebody yelled, "First base!" The runner who had been on first thought the ball was going to drop in and he had gone a long way off the bag toward second. So I threw across my body toward first to try to double him off and—poong!—something pulled in my side. It was a muscle tear along the ribs. If you have ever broken a rib, you know what the pain is like. Well, this was just about the same. I couldn't take a deep breath or make any sudden moves. Worse than that, I couldn't swing a bat. It might have cleared up in a few days except that every morning when I wake up I sneeze—probably because of a sort of mild asthma that I have. When I sneezed I'd tear that muscle again. It took a couple of weeks to heal enough so that I could swing a bat freely.

When I got back in the lineup, everything was fine for a while. I started feeling strong again, and began hitting. As the season went into June I began to feel that this might be the one—the good season without too much trouble physically. Then one rainy night in Baltimore, chasing a home run ball that Brooks Robinson hit just over the center field fence, I ran into the chain-link fence out there and broke a bone in my left foot. I was out from early June until late July. When I got back to the point where I could run a little and swing the bat, I felt something wrong with my left knee. I remembered that on the night I broke my foot I had a lump on my knee, too, but I didn't think too much about it at the time. But in late July came the bad news, for the third time that year. I was stuck on the sideline until things healed up. I had to take it easy most of the rest of that season, and really didn't get to play all out until September, just before the World Series. After the Series I had to have an operation on the knee. (I have been in hospitals so often I'm beginning to feel like a doctor.) In the meantime my nice healthy season had gone down the drain.

All the talk about my injuries and my difficulties is to get you to realize that *nobody* has it easy all the time. Even the life of a major league ballplayer can be awfully rough at times. Being Mickey Mantle is great when you get your bat on a fast ball and hit a game-winning home run. I have had moments like that, and am grateful for them. They are what I dreamed about when I was a boy. I have had the privilege of knowing what it feels like to have my dreams come true.

But with the dreams that come true, there is also pain and heartache and plain hard work. Nothing is easy, except when you work hard at it. Nobody worked harder at learning everything there is to know about hitting than Ted Williams, and nobody works harder on pitching than Whitey Ford.

Or take Willie Mays. Willie makes everything look easy. He makes everything look like fun. He so seldom makes a bad play that he makes playing baseball seem like a breeze. But what he does *looks* easy only because it is so hard to do. It's like watching a trapeze artist at the circus or an acrobat or even a magician doing card tricks. We applaud a difficult trick when it looks hard, but we laugh with pleasure and delight when it looks easy.

That's the way Willie does it. But don't think it's easy to do just because it looks easy. I can't forget that Willie collapsed and passed out on the bench during ball games a couple of times a season or two back. When the doctors examined him they said he was suffering from utter exhaustion. Willie had been driving himself so hard that he had literally worn himself out. But figure it out. You have to work hard to be able to make things look as easy as Willie makes them look.

Doing something well may seem like fun, but it isn't easy to make yourself work hard to learn how to do it. It is fun to work hard when everything is going your way, but it's no fun at all—and I know it—when everything seems to be going against you. It's fun to do a difficult job if it's something you enjoy, like football, for instance, but it's awfully tough to stick to it when it's something you don't like to do, like studying. Even when it's something that you know will help you in the long run.

The toughest game, the hardest fight, anything at all, can get to be a challenge that you really enjoy when everybody is rooting for you and cheering you on. But when it seems as though everybody and everything is against you—well, it takes guts to hang in there. It takes heart. It takes courage.

But if *you* want something, if *you* want to be somebody, *you* have to have it. You have to hang on. You have to come through.

It isn't easy, but you can do it. I know you can.